COMING OF AGE IN THE WEST 1883 - 1906

From the Mississippi to California and
Gold Rush Alaska
with my Minister Father, 1883-1906

A Memoir by WILL E. GURR

Edited and Annotated by

TED ROBERT GURR

with an Account of his Uncle's Life

on Lake Chelan, 1906 - 1977

ISBN: 1456326074
ISBN-13: 9781456326074

Printed by CreateSpace, An Amazon.com Company

CONTENTS

A Note on the Photos

All photos are contemporary and only one has been published elsewhere. Many are from the Rev. Henry J. Gurr's three surviving albums, noted *HJG* on the photo captions. One of the albums says that
they were "taken with the Blair camera and films." Others are from
Will E. Gurr's "lost album," found by Barbara Van Epps in 2011, or
surviving postcards. These are noted *WEG album.* A third group is
from the Lake Chelan Historical Museum, coded *LCHM.* One of these,
an early 20th century panoramic view of Chelan, has been used by the
Museum in its publications. Two are century-old studio photographs
of the Gurrs. The 1917 photo of Will Gurr and Art Campbell in swim
suits is a copy of an enlargement that hangs next to reception in the
Campbell Hotel in Chelan and is reproduced with the Campbell family's permission. Two other photos are from the editor's collection.
The photos were restored by Lorie K. Zirbes of Las Vegas (http://
retouching bylorie.com) who was an invaluable source of expertise
on retouching, cropping, and printing old photos.

Figure

Photos

PREFACE AND ACKNOWLEDGEMENTS

Will Gurr had an extraordinary childhood and adolescence. After his mother's death in 1887, when he was four, Will and his older brother were uprooted from their California home by their grieving father, the London-born Episcopal clergyman Henry Jonathan Gurr. He took them first to England and back, then to a dozen towns and parishes in California, the upper Midwest and the Mississippi, the Colorado Rockies, and Alaska during the Gold Rush. Will saw the 1893 Chicago World's Fair and visited Kelly's Army of unemployed workers as they camped on the banks of the Mississippi in 1894. He lived, travelled, and worked in Alaska Territory from 1898 to 1906, with vivid memories of Skagway, Juneau, Sitka, and sailing on the Inside Passage.

Will was "almost an orphan," in the words of my cousin and collaborator Paul Magel. He and his brother's longest residence during a decade of wandering was two years in a boarding home in San Mateo, where their father placed them after he "went broke." He married twice more but Will had no love and little care from either of his stepmothers. His resilient character was formed partly by his minister father but mainly through his experiences as he learned to make his own way in the world.

The Rev. Gurr's quest for gold and adventure brought them to Alaska in late 1898. He and the boys outfitted a schooner in San Francisco and almost lost their lives in storm-shortened efforts to sail north. Once in Alaska by steamer, they made a harrowing early-winter trip over the White Pass and across British Columbia's lakes to a gold strike in Atlin. Here, at the age of 15, Will chose to go on his own. For the next seven years he lived in coastal Alaska, growing from a stubborn and rebellious boy into an accomplished and self-confident young man who could set type, run a launch for charter, travel and hunt in the wilderness, and work as a Federal jail guard.

The heart of this book consists of Will's memoirs of his boyhood, written when he was in his 70s and titled "Life of a Minister's Son." They are told as a series of escapades, adventures and misadventures. He had few complaints about the hazards of his youth nor does he reflect much on the character or decisions of his restless father. Beneath the narrative, though, the reader can see the maturation of a competent and determined young man with a strong moral compass. Those were evident in the subsequent 70 years during which Will was a leading citizen of Chelan, a lakeside town on the eastern edge of Washington State's Cascade Mountains. The last part of this book is my account of his life in Chelan, a life in which he played many parts as a businessman, a community activist as we would call him today, mayor, nature photographer, constable and judge, and husband.

Paul Magel and Elizabeth Watson Perry have made invaluable contributions to this book. Paul has done diligent research on the life and times of our common ancestors, the three Gurr brothers of London. Liz Perry, a Chelan native, has done extensive research and writing on the history of the Chelan valley and its residents. She also suggested the phrase "Coming of Age in the West" that I have used as the book's title. Both Paul and Liz have been generous in sharing the results of their research with me. Several of Paul's contributions are included and credited in the text.

My brother David shares my fascination with our family's adventuresome history and has supported this project throughout. Our mother, Anne Gurr, and our cousin Father Jack Gurr, SJ, saved and passed on some of Will's late-life correspondence. Both died long before they knew what use I would make of the documentation. Jessica Flaggs, a student assistant at the University of Maryland, worked painstakingly to transcribe the tattered typescript of Will's memoirs into a computer file. My daughter Lisa Anne Gurr offered a cultural anthropologist's perspective on the project. Suellen Pirages provided a useful critical reading of the draft manuscript. Late in the project Barbara Van Epps of Chelan wrote down her childhood memories of "Grandpa Bill," who had married her widowed grandmother in 1954. They offer invaluable details about his personality and his life in Chelan and are quoted at length in the last section.

The book is illustrated with photos from the Rev. Gurr's albums from the 1890s to 1910, from the archives of the Lake Chelan Historical Society's museum, and from a family album provided by Barbara Van Epps. Thanks to Liz Perry and her colleague at the museum, Roberta Simonds, for searching out and scanning their photos. Lorie K. Zirbes of Las Vegas (http://retouching bylorie.com) worked wonders in restoring the photos and preparing them for publication.

Barbara Harff deserves special thanks for tolerating her husband's quixotic efforts to bring this project to fruition.

Coming of Age in the West 1883 -1906

FAMILY CONNECTIONS

Me and Uncle Will

The first visit I remember to Chelan was in summer, probably 1940. My father, Robert Lucas Gurr, drove west from Spokane in our gray Chevy sedan, stopping in Grand Coulee to watch construction on the dam, nearly a mile wide, that would eventually provide power and irrigation for much of central Washington State. We drove another 50 miles across arid badlands and lava flats to Chelan Falls on the Columbia River and turned north a few miles up the Chelan River to the town. Chelan occupies a splendid site at the southern end of a narrow glacier-carved lake of the same name that slices 55 miles northwest into the heart of the North Cascade mountains. The lake ends at a glacial moraine where the resort village of Stehekin is the only settlement in a rugged and mostly uninhabited wilderness area, so isolated that Stehekin was not connected to the state telephone grid until 2007.

Chelan's 1500 residents in 1940 lived on the trade of orchardists and ranchers in the surrounding valleys and supplied the handful of loggers and miners who worked up-lake. In summer tourists would arrive from Wenatchee, Spokane and Seattle to stay at the Campbell Hotel in town, or to take the *Lady of the Lake* to the lodge at Stehekin. By 2010 the population increased, but only to 4000, and the town enjoys some modest prosperity because of the surrounding orchards and vineyards. The lake's microclimate is well-suited to viniculture and a few wineries and wine bars have opened in recent years. Will Gurr would have welcomed the prosperity but probably not the wine because, as he observes near the end of his memoirs, he never liked alcohol.

Our destination was my Uncle Will's home.[1] I have a dim memory of a tall and slender man of middle age with a voice deeper than my father's. I slept on a screened porch and awoke to Uncle Will's singing wakeup call: "Cantaloupe for breakfast, honey and a bun, get your shoes and stockings on and run, run, run!" It was my first experience with the juicy orange fruit and I followed my uncle's lead by sprinkling mine with a little salt to bring out the sweetness. He said he learned the ditty from his father, a London-born clergyman - who may also have been in the habit of salting his fruit.

As a boy I knew little about Uncle Will and even less of his father, the Rev. Henry J. Gurr. But stories were told and old photos and a few other treasures were passed on, hinting that these men and their families had led unusual lives.[2] On one family visit to Chelan Will Gurr pointed out, from his front lawn, the promontory on Bear Mountain, eight miles up the lake, where his father had built the homestead he called "Gurrland" early in the 20th century. In town was St. Andrew's Episcopal Church, since 1992 on the National Register of Historical Sites, a log structure where the Rev. Gurr had preached for nearly 20 years.

In the early 1950s, before I went to college, Will gave me a beautiful jewelers' balance scale and a set of brass weights in a glass-fronted hardwood case, a relic of the jewelry store he had sold a few years earlier. When he heard that I had kept it, he insisted that it was to be sold and the proceeds used for college costs. So I sold it for $30 or so to a jeweler in Spokane and bought a black 1938 Pontiac sedan that got me to college in Portland and back.[3] And in the 1960s, after I had gone East to take a university position, my mother forwarded

---

1   Christened William, the family always called him Will. As a boy in Alaska he was Billie, in Chelan usually Bill.

2   One treasure was a memento of the Rev. Gurr's years at sea as a youth and later along the southern Alaska coast: a bronze collapsing telescope that was stored under the Chevy's seats but forgotten when the car was sold.

3   The money stayed in the family because I bought the car from my mother's nephew, "Vinegar Bill" Exworthy, a logger and white-water rafter. His ramshackle house and collection of junked vehicles near the center of Priest River, Idaho, offended the city fathers, but they could do nothing so long as he had evidence that it was a used car business. I got the best of the lot.

at Will's request a flimsy carbon copy of a 35-page typescript, "Life of a Minister's Son." In it Will set out his recollections of his first 23 years as the son of an itinerant minister, with a vivid vernacular account of adventures in 1890s California and Alaska during and after the Gold Rush. A potential book, I thought, even though the account ended abruptly when Will left Alaska in 1906 to settle in Chelan.

Since then I have continued to accumulate evidence to round out the story of Will and the other Gurrs who settled in Chelan – how they lived, where and why they traveled so widely, who they married and left behind. The homesteads established on Bear Mountain by the Rev. Gurr and his younger brother Edwin Robert, who followed him from London, were too high, dry, and far from town to be sustainable. Almost all ranches in the First Creek district, including Bear Mountain, have been abandoned, some of them reverting to public ownership.[4] Where private land remains on Bear Mountain, developers are promoting a golf course and new homes. Nature has reclaimed the saddle where Gurrland stood. Will Gurr said that the house was used by hunters for many years but burned one winter in the 1940s. Its foundations are now buried beneath new-growth pines that screen the spectacular view up the lake. A few water-stressed lilacs and Virginia creepers mark what was probably the front stoop. Scattered sawn timbers nearby are the likely site of the barn while 100 yard SE the remains of the root cellar can be seen, dug into the slope facing Chelan town. And a radio relay station now sits near the edge of the 1600-foot cliff that looks NE toward Wapato Point and the town of Manson. Will's nephew Robert Gurr, who grew up at Gurrland, recalled that one of the family's precious cows died in a fall over the cliff.

The central part of this book is an edited version of Will Gurr's memoirs of his youth, followed by my account of his life in Chelan. He arrived in 1906 and during the next 70 years there became one of the town's leading citizens. He owned a jewelry business on Woodin Avenue for 41 years, a street that has preserved its appearance in the 1930's – now graced with plantings. As a young man Will pitched

---

4   Elizabeth Watson Perry recounts the history of this area in *"We Left Because the Creek Went Dry": The People of the First Creek District Lake Chelan, Washington 1888-1932* (Wenatchee: Cascade Graphics, 1999).

for the local baseball team and founded the town's fire department. He married two local women and outlived both. He also served as mayor, council member, deputy sheriff, justice of the peace, and municipal judge before his death in 1977, aged 93. When I visited the Chelan Rotary Club 30 years later, in autumn 2007, only a handful of people recognized his name.

The Parents and the Brothers Gurr[5]

Will's character and early life adventures were inheritances from his father, the Rev. Henry J. Gurr. He was born in west London in 1853, the second of three sons of Alfred James and Mary Gurr. Alfred, whose parents came from a village in the South Downs of East Sussex,[6] exemplified the rising lower middle classes of Victorian Britain. The son of a publican, he was a butler at the time of Henry J.'s birth but in a few years went into retail trade as a dairyman, importing and distributing milk to a network of customers in the vicinity of Paddington Station. The business prospered, so much so that it provided employment and a comfortable income to his sons and three daughters – all of whom worked in the firm at one time or another.

Henry J. was sent to a private school until, at age 15, he went to sea as a cabin boy. His years at sea, said to be mainly in the India trade, gave him the skills of a sailor and a life-long love of adventure. He worked at the family business in the 1870s but by the age of 22 was back at sea. He worked his way to Duluth, Minnesota, on a cargo ship and, beginning in fall 1876, was enrolled in the Episcopal

---

5   This account of Will Gurr's life is part of a larger biographical and social history project on the Gurr brothers and their families. Already published is "Daily Life in Chelan in 1911: From the Diary of Capt. John B. Lucas," by Ted Robert Gurr and Elizabeth Watson Perry, in *Lake Chelan History Notes*, vol. XX (2005), pp. 30-39. John Lucas, a Crimean War veteran and immigrant from England, was the father of Mabel Lucas Gurr, the Rev. Gurr's third wife and mother of their five children, most of them – including my father - born in Chelan and raised at the Gurrland ranch. In an as-yet-unpublished ms. I trace the life of Will's father: "' A Restless and Not Very Practical Man': The Reverend Henry J. Gurr in Chelan, 1902 – 1921." This will be incorporated in a detailed account of the Gurr brothers' English origins, London life, and emigration to North America that is being prepared by Paul Magel, a great grandson of the Rev. Gurr's younger brother, Edward Robert.

6   The Gurr family name is first recorded in the 16th century and almost all early references are from villages in South Sussex and West Kent, along the old road leading north from Hastings. Genealogical and linguistic research by Paul Magel suggests that the Gurr name is of the same provenance as the common French surname Guerre and the even more common Spanish Guerra. The origin of the English word "war" is guerre (from Old French) and the related word guerrier means "warrior" or "foot soldier" in both old and modern French. "The first Gurr" was probably a retainer of one of the Anglo-Norman barons who had estates in southern England and who, in the 13th and 14th centuries, led men in battle to defend English territory in northern France.

Church's Seabury Divinity School in Faribault, Minnesota. Ordained in 1879, he served for several years at churches in Minnesota.

In Willmar, Minnesota, Henry J. met and married Celia Frost, the daughter of a physician. Will said in later years that her family was descended from Loyalists, 38,000 or so of whom fled to Canada during the American Revolution. Celia herself was born in St. John, New Brunswick. By the 1870s, perhaps a little earlier, the Frosts had emigrated south to Minnesota. We know little of the Frosts' life but they evidently prospered. According to Will his mother was a graduate of the Boston Conservatory of Music and her sister lived in New York. The accompanying family tree shows the relationships among the members of the Gurr clan mentioned here and in Will's memoirs.

Celia and Henry had two sons, Alfred born in 1881 and William in 1883, children of a marriage that Henry J. later said from the pulpit was as close to heaven as he had ever gotten in this life. She became ill, though, so the young family left Whapeton, North Dakota, in March 1884 to resettle in the West, first in Portland and shortly thereafter in Centerville, now Fremont, southeast of Oakland. Celia died in October 1887 and during the next 15 years the Rev. Henry J. traveled incessantly with his two sons, first back to London, then to a dozen or more parishes as distant from one another as Warsaw, Illinois, on the Mississippi, Buena Vista in the Colorado mining country, and Juneau during the Gold Rush. The boys had little choice but to go along, even when he had to leave them for two years in a boy's home in San Mateo. Their father's brief second marriage came and went with little effect on them. Nor were they close to Mabel Lucas, his third and much younger wife, with whom he had five more children. By the age of 15 Will had enough of the nomadic life and parted company with his father to winter alone in a cabin they had built in Atlin, in the interior of British Columbia.

There were nonetheless family ties that led both brothers to travel from Alaska to Chelan, Washington, where their father and Mabel finally settled down in 1902. After several such trips Alf returned to Alaska and settled in coastal Alaska where he worked as a banker. He married a Roman Catholic woman and their children, John and Cecilia, both joined Catholic orders. Cecilia became

Mother Superior of a girl's school in Oregon. John (Father Jack to all who knew and worked with him) became a Jesuit theologian, a university professor and dean. He returned to his beloved Alaska to serve as a priest on the North Slope pipeline and as parish priest in Bethel, a village near the mouth of the Kuskokwim River. His life, as adventuresome in its own way as Will Gurr's, deserves its own biography.

Figure 1. The Gurr Families from London to America

This attenuated family history highlights the descendants of the three Gurr brothers mentioned in "Coming of Age in the West." The brothers were sons of **Alfred James Gurr** (1824-74) and **Mary Ann Bennett** (1820-84) who also had three daughters.

Immigrants to the US from London	Marriages and Children	The Next Two Generations
Alfred Richard Gurr, 1851-1944, and Emily Hunter, 1854-1940, emigrated 1889 to Merced with 12 children	Edwin **(Ted)** 1877, was their third child, Mary **(Maud)** 1880, their fifth	
Henry Jonathan Gurr, 1853-1931, emigrated 1875, graduated from Episcopal divinity school in Faribault, Minnesota, 1879	**Henry Jonathan** *married 1880, Minnesota* **Celia Spurr Frost,** 1853-1887. Two sons: **Alfred (Alf),** 1881-1961 **William E. (Will)** 1883-1977	**Alf Gurr** *married c. 1912,* Helena Mary Resided in coastal Alaska. Two children: **John (Father Jack), SJ** 1913-94 **Cecilia (Sister Cecilia)** 1914-89
Henry Jonathan was ordained in 1879 and ministered in the Midwest, West, and Alaska until 1902	**Henry Jonathan** *Married 1888, London* **Alice Gardner,** 1868- *Divorced 1894, California* No children	**Will Gurr** *Married 1909, Chelan* **Maude Pruitt,** 1888-1952. No children *Married 1957, Chelan* **Gladys Waring Gibson,** 1893-1963
Henry Jonathan moved to Chelan in 1902 and ministered there for almost twenty years. He homesteaded on Bear Mountain alongside his brother Edwin	**Henry Jonathan** *married 1897, Chicago* **Mabel Lucas,** 1875-1940, daughter of **Capt. John Lucas,** Five children, including **Robert Lucas** 1905-80	**Robert Lucas Gurr** *Married 1926, Spokane* **Anne Cook,** 1902-1998 Two sons: **Ted Robert Gurr,** 1936- **David Gurr,** 1940-
Edwin Robert (Teddy) Gurr, 1855-1929, emigrated in 1893 to Merced with Alice and two sons. He returned to London when Alice died, moved to Chelan in 1907	**Teddy Gurr** *married 1887, London* Alice Santer, 1864-1894, died Merced **Teddy Gurr** *married 1903 Portsmouth* Ada Hall, 1855-1935	George Herbert Gurr was the eldest son of Teddy and Alice. He emigrated to Winnipeg in 1905. His grandson is **Paul Albert Magel,** 1936-

Alf is a major character in Will's memoirs, as much so as his father. Mabel is mentioned along with her father, Captain John Lucas. A cousin, Ted Gurr, also makes a brief appearance. He was a son of Henry J.'s older brother, Alfred Richard, who emigrated from London with his wife and 12 children in 1889 and settled in Merced, California. Later in life Will corresponded frequently with Father Jack and with Robert and Anne Gurr. Robert was born in Chelan in 1906, the second child and first son of Henry J. and Mabel. He and his wife Anne (the editor's parents) frequently visited and corresponded with Will in Chelan. The third and youngest Gurr brother, Edward Robert Gurr, has a kind of ghostly presence in Will's life. He followed his older brothers to America, homesteaded on Bear Mountain next to Gurrland and assuredly was known to Will, even though he is never mentioned by name in the memoirs or correspondence. He was the great-grandfather of Paul Magel, with whom I have worked closely in tracing the history of the Gurr clan.

The account of Will Gurr's life that follows aims to suggest something of the motives and character of people who traveled and settled in the American West. In his memoirs Will says with some regret that he wished he could meet and speak again with some of his school teachers. "I would not have a bright and shining career to hold up before them, however I would aim to convince them that tho I had kicked life away, yet how much I had appreciated their efforts." In retrospect Will did not kick his life away. Neither he nor his father or uncles gained wealth or wide renown in North America. Yet they were not "ordinary people." On the contrary, the brothers left behind a prosperous family business in London, moved often, worked many jobs and trades – often simultaneously, survived hardship and ill health with resilience, and took risks that from the perspective of 21st century American life may seem foolhardy and doomed to failure. They kept up their family ties and helped and looked after many people in their public and private lives. Yet none of them, least of all Will, expressed any regrets. What follows is Will's life's story, much of it in his own words.

WILL GURR'S MEMOIRS 1883 - 1906

Edited and annotated by Ted Robert Gurr

Will Gurr's account of his first 23 years, a faded carbon copy of a typescript, is undated but evidently was written in the 1960s. Its original title is "Life of a Minister's Son." Born in Whapeton, North Dakota in 1883, he made his home in Chelan, Washington from 1907 until his death on May 12, 1977. I thank Jessica Flaggs, a research assistant at the University of Maryland, for transcribing the carbon copy. The copy has the notation "Will Gurr gave me this in June 1969," in the hand of Anne Gurr, my mother and his sister-in-law.

Will wrote multiple versions of some pages and I have selected what appear to be the later versions, or in some cases have combined elements of both. He also writes without much concern for continuity. So in some instances, especially his recollections of life and work in Juneau, I have organized his accounts by theme and temporal sequence. The subheadings in the text are also my addition along with many paragraph breaks. I have corrected a few obvious spelling errors and fixed punctuation problems. Some repetitive phrases are eliminated. For example Will often begins an account with "I will never forget..." and includes successive sentences that begin "Finally...." I have eliminated some such redundant phrases. He capitalizes Father and Mother and I have retained this usage. His inconsistent references to his Brother Alf or Bro, with or without capitalization, have been left unchanged. Otherwise the text is inclusive and in his own vernacular. My and Paul Magel's comments and annotations, both those in the text and footnotes, are in italics.

My daughter Lisa Anne Gurr, a cultural anthropologist, says that any changes to Will Gurr's text distort his voice. The account that follows thus is not exactly what he said, but what I as an editor think he wanted to say. She is correct. Since some readers may want to read his original, I will deposit three documents with the Lake Chelan Historical Society. One is a copy of Will's original carbon. Second is a CD with Jessica Flag's exact transcription of the carbon-copy document, including a few elisions where she could not decipher the original. Last is an electronic copy of the text that follows. The compare-text function in a word processing program will allow another researcher to see where and how I have modified Will's account. I wish he were here to approve and correct what I have done with his narrative.

– TRG January 2011

LIFE OF A MINISTER'S SON

According to a diary which my Father had kept in bygone days, I was born at Wahpeton, N. D., although for two reasons I cannot verify this. I was too young for one, the other was they never kept records until about six years after I was born. His diary showed that I was born October, 16, 1883 but until I was about twenty-three I celebrated my birthday on the fifteenth. It was not until I came to Chelan on a visit that my step-mother said that in going through an old diary of my fathers, it showed that I was born on the 16th. So I proceeded to change the date of my arrival, in fact had always had a desire to have split the month in two, though I cannot say it has benefited me in any way, on the other I guess it has not hurt me either.

Childhood Memories and My Mother's Death

When I was about ten months old my Father took my Mother, brother Alf, and myself to Portland, Ore. In a letter which my Mother wrote to her sister in New York, she told how scared she was, crossing the ferry on the Columbia, stating that it was pretty poor make-shift transportation. We did not stay there long before my Father decided it was too rainy and damp for my Mother's health, so he left there and we went to Centerville, Alameda Co., California.[7]

I remember one time when they were having company. There was a young lady serving dinner who brought in two pastry pies and put them on the table. I can hear my Dad today say, "Why what's this?" and she said, "Well when I put them in the pantry they were all right and when I went to get them they were like this." Some little devil, not mentioning any names, had gone in there and stuck his finger in

---

[7]   Centerville, later renamed Fremont, is north of San Jose at the southeast end of San Francisco Bay. The Rev. Henry J. Gurr was pastor in St. James Church in Centerville. A testimonial in his records from church officials says that he served there for five years, though that service was at best intermittent. Centerville is about 80 miles west and slightly north of Merced in the Central Valley, discussed later in this memoir.

each one just to taste them. Dad looked over at me, excused himself, came over, picked me up and played the drums on the seat of my pants, and for some reason or other I lost all interest in pastry pies.

It was there that we lost her and oh God, how I was to miss her later on. I can very well remember one day when Mother was confined to her bed, she had my brother on her right and I was on her left when Father came into the room. I remember oh so well him saying, "Oh Celia you should not do that" and she replied, "Oh I want to". It was a just a few days after that when I went into the room, and the bed was empty, but not made up. I opened another door leading into the main room, and it was filled with ladies sitting around the room on benches.

I remember one time when my Dad asked my brother if he had done something, tho I do not know what is was, however he said he did not do it, so my Dad came over, picked me up and was about half through whipping me when my brother said he did it. I do not think my Dad gave him a licking. I guess he figured as long as he had been honest enough to own up to it he would not whip him for it.

I will never forget one time I went over to the church and opened the front door. There was a round glass window in front of the church, up near the apex of the roof. Some boy had evidently broken it and a big hoot owl had gone into the church unbeknownst to me. When I opened that door and stepped inside he let out a hoot, and I just about went through the door and never stopped until I reached the rectory next door. I think I would have made some runners sit up and take notice how I burned up the ground getting away from there.

The Rail Journey West, Spring 1884:
Letters from Celia Gurr

The Richland County Gazette *of March 28, 1884, reported on the circumstances that led the Rev. Henry Gurr to move his family from Whapeton to the West Coast.* "Mrs. Gurr's health had been poor before they took up their residence in this city. Since then her lungs have troubled her quite seriously until by the advice of physicians they decided to leave for California hoping a warmer climate would enable her to gain in health strength. But we were [concerned] that she would not live to perform the journey." *These are two letters that Celia wrote to her mother about their journey on the Northern Pacific Railroad.*

Pyramid Park Sleeper
Bismark, Sunday, March 30th, 1884

ᑎᗢ

My dear Mother,

Instead of being in San Francisco we are still in Dacotah. We left Moorhead Friday morning and arrived here in the evening where we have had to remain on account of the Missouri being blocked with ice and the track covered with water. Some of the passengers were transferred across the river in small boats, to take the train on the other side at their own risks. Our car is quite full of passengers waiting as we are.

Harry took a statement-room or drawing-room for fifty dollars and it is really worth a hundred to us. [*This was a considerable extravagance for a country clergyman. The Rev. Gurr was a member of the Whapeton lodge of the IOOF whose members gave him a farewell testimonial and a check for $71.50, part of which he probably used to pay for the drawing room. Transcriptions of the newspaper article and testimonial were preserved in his papers, along with copies of Celia's letters.*] We are entirely to ourselves with plenty of room to eat and rest. Yesterday the baby [*Will, aged 5 months*] was sick but I thought nothing of it until evening

Celia Frost Gurr, undated   *HJG*

Alf and Will as children, ca. 1885   *HJG*

when his stomach was like touching a lump of ice and his bowels seemed to knot into hard lumps. The poor little fellow cried hard in spite of all the jumping, walking, and all one could do.

Three ladies came to the door to ask if they could not do something to relieve us and one of them walked him for a long time. Harry and I fussed over him all night, wringing out flannel in alcohol and hot water, and Harry gave him medicine every two hours. This morning he is sleeping quietly and taking his milk – he did not have an hour's sleep yesterday....

I will send you a picture of our room so you can imagine how beautifully we are situated. We would have plenty of room for you if you were only with us – we have two lower and two upper berths.

I am feeling much better and this seems such a pleasant rest. We get our own meals as it costs seventy-five cents to buy them! Harry bought a spirit lamp yesterday and we make our own coffee, boil eggs, etc., and have canned tongue and boiled ham. Some of them have their lunch with them and others go to the hotel – the dining-room car they took back to St. Paul yesterday morning. We may get away by Tuesday and perhaps sooner.

Bismarck is quite a pretty place and Valley City and Jamestown are situated as prettily as I would wish. It looks like very high hills and valleys all throughout the country. Opposite the Missouri here the bluffs look like Houston Co. bluffs. Alfie *[aged three]* is writing away on the other side of the table. I ask him if I should send his letter to Ma and he looks very pleased as he answers yes. He eats anything now and enjoys his meals. He sleeps splendidly at night. I took him for a little walk yesterday and he enjoyed everything very much, particularly one of those Indians with outstretched arm and cigars in his hand which is used as a sign for a cigar shop....

I am so glad I have on my black dress as so many things get spilt on it. Does it not seem grand to have my traveling dress all fresh and two black silks? *[The last two paragraphs are family greetings.]*

Your affectionate daughter, Celia

ᐭ

Portland, Oregon
April 4. 1884

My dear Mother,

We have all arrived safe and well so far on our journey, it would not have seemed at all tiresome or tedious but for our having to wait from Friday till Monday and then being transferred across the river to Mandan....We should have arrived here last Tuesday instead of Friday, which is today. The baby is looking well but still troubled with diarrhea. I do not know how we should possibly have managed without the drawing-room – it is so secluded that one can do anything without the eyes of the passengers being fastened on one.

I have not seen one bit of country since we left Jamestown that I would want to live in. Montana, Idaho, and Washington Territory is one vast barren, desolate looking waste. We had one afternoon of grand scenery in Montana but that was going up over the mountains, the only place I have seen any woods the long journey through. The trip was nothing, I would go the same distance anytime only for the money and that does not seem very much. I think we take the steamer tomorrow evening for San Francisco.

I felt afraid that we would not get our trunks for a month by the looks of the *[Missouri]* river, but they said they took the luggage across day before yesterday. The water was fully two miles and a half wide – we crossed a very long bridge in the train and then were rowed a mile and a quarter. My heart just ached for the poor immigrants. One poor woman's baby died in the depot at Mandan and was taken away the morning we got there. She looked very sad and I could not but be thankful that it was not our baby who had gone. The family were going East instead of West, though. I looks queer to see them going in that direction, yet I should not like any part of the Western territories I have seen. I suppose the Northern Pacific does not travel through the better parts. We saw any amount of Indians with their blankets on, their huts were very numerous but the Chinese *[brought in to build the railroad]* are worse than the Indians – their huts were just the same and their way of living cannot be very different.

We got here this morning at half-past six, exactly a week on the road when we should have been four days. It is very warm here, the grass bright green, and there are tulips in blossom in the garden opposite. We have fires throughout the hotel. I gave the baby a bath and changed his clothes directly after breakfast....Alfie is asleep – he takes a nap everyday and has a splendid appetite. Willie is asleep too. Harry has gone to see Bishop Morris. I will close this and if I have any more news will write after Harry comes.

Very much love to you all, your affectionate daughter, Celia

To London

After some months my Father left Centerville. We went back to Minnesota where my Mother's brother, Dr. Edward Spurr Frost, was a physician and surgeon, and where my brother had been born in 1881. We stayed there for a while and then left for London, England, where Dad was born, stopping on the way in New York City where my Mother's sister lived.

I do not know how long we stayed in New York, however I do not think very long. I remember London quite well, tho I do not remember any of the trip over. When we arrived there I remember one evening my cousin Maud, one of a family of ten children, razzed me about having taken my mug to drink out of. I did not like the way she said it, so took it away from her, she put out a squeal and her mother came over and took it away from me and gave it back to her. She razzed me again with the same thing happening so I took it away from her again and wound up in a dark closet. She was the only cousin that I really did not seem to get along with, and later on in California we tangled again, tho her mother was not there to take her part.[8] Well do I also remember one night when we were saying our prayers and when we came to the words, "God bless Papa and Mama," my brother broke down and cried. I can remember one of my aunts comforting him and saying, "Oh he misses his Mother."

One day my Father went over to France and left me behind. I was upstairs in the bedroom and I surely whooped it up. My two aunts came up and evidently comforted me and I undoubtedly lived through it as here I am today.[9]

One day Father took my brother and myself to Scotland. We came to a park, a beautiful green rolling piece of landscape covered with well-kept grass, through which a path wound its way. On one side of the path was a little guard house with a big burly Scotchman stand-

---

8 *Maud was Alfred Richard's daughter Mary Maud Gurr, born in 1880 and thus about three years older than Will.*

9 *The aunts were Alfred Richard's wife Emily and Edward Robert's first wife Alice (nee Santer). Evidently all three families were sharing the same dwelling.*

ing in front of it, dressed in kilts, with his fancy plaid outfit. I could not help but wonder at the time if he was quite uncomfortable, with his kilt and short stockings, as it was a little on the raw and cool side.

I remember one evening my brother and myself went with our cousins to a small and narrow park not very far from where we were living. A boy came along whose father ran a business in competition to theirs and they poked fun at him. He jumped the fence and started after them leaving poor little me behind. I set up a howl that I think would have made a coyote sit up and take notice, but he came up to me and said he would not hurt me as I hadn't done anything. So that was another time when I lived to breathe some more.

The English houses have as a general rule high rock walls on both sides of the lot, with a gate and different fences at the rear. My brother and myself had to amuse ourselves as best we could and I remember one day he was digging up worms, then cutting them in two to see if they would join, when a lady next door stood on a chair and asked us if we would mind being quiet, as someone was sick at her home. We evidently were as later on she appeared at the fence with a plate of dates which she passed over to us.

From London to San Diego

I do not know how long we were in England, however I remember the boat well that we came back to the U.S. on. It was the worst rolling, floundering old boat that I ever rode on. I remember one morning I had just come out of our stateroom and the waiters had the table all set for breakfast, when the old girl gave a roll and all the dishes slid onto the floor. The waiters finally got the mess cleaned up and put the racks on the table, after which we had breakfast, however that storm lasted for three days. My Father fastened a rope to the wall and to our bunk so that we would not fall out of the upper berth.

Coming over there was a Dutch family traveling steerage with a little boy about six. His Dad would fill a pipe full of tobacco, light it and hand it to the boy who would stand and smoke it like an old hand. His Dad seemed to be quite proud of the boy's ability, and he was quite an attraction to the passengers.

After landing at New York we went down south, then through New Mexico and up to San Diego, Cal. *[The crossing was in the winter of 1888-89, the arrival in San Diego early in 1889.]* I will never forget that country, you could travel for miles upon mile, then perhaps come upon a Mexican dobio *[adobe]* I think they are called. I remember one night we pulled into a station where there was a water tank. The railroad bed was built up about four foot high, evidently to keep it from getting covered with sand. Parallel to the railroad track and about 150 yards away was a row of old one-story, dilapidated business buildings which looked as tho they might have seen better days about 70 years back. My Father and brother went out on the depot platform but I stayed in my seat. Two Indians came along the track, one dressed in a leather outfit with leather fringes on the pants legs, one of the younger generation, from one direction, and from the other an old Indian with nothing on but a breech clout and a dagger sticking in the clout. They met right under the window where I was looking out. They entered into a conversation, and while they were talking the young fellow reached down and picked up an old cigar butt, evidently thrown out the window by a passenger, said something to the old Indian and offered it to him. But the old Indian did not seem to appreciate the joke, as he whipped out his knife and said something to the young Indian who reached into his pocket, pulled out what change he had, which was less than a dollar, and handed it to the old Indian, They parted and went back the ways they had come. I asked my Dad how these Indians and Mexicans made a living, he said keeping up the railroad tracks,

In our coach there were only six of us, another man and his two sons, about our ages. I remember him showing Dad where he had shot buffalo and sold them to the railroad. I also vividly remember the frozen cattle, killed by the last storm.

When we arrived in San Diego and got off the train, Dad gave the colored porter a tip. When Dad came over to us he said, "There goes my last dollar." I asked, why did you give it to him, his answer was, "He was so good to us."

Broke in California and Two Years in a Boys' Home

We stayed in San Diego for awhile, then took a steamer to Frisco. I do not think we were there long before Dad went broke I remember late one night we arrived at a two story, square brick building, where you went up about seven steps to the front door. Dad left my brother and myself outside, then came out and took us in. It was a school for boys, not far from San Mateo.[10] We were shown into a room where there were several boys in bed and we were given a couple of cots. Morning call came fairly early, we washed, dressed and then all filed down to breakfast, no sugar or butter and very poor milk with some times wormy oatmeal. One morning we were given some sugar and some other ration and tho I forget what it was, it was interesting to see boys trading with one another.

We were not allowed to talk at the table. One evening I whispered, was called out on the floor and told to hold out my hand, and received four or five smacks across the palm of my hand with a one-inch stick. Another evening I had a great big boiled onion which had not even been salted put in front of me. I could not to eat it. Mrs. L came along and told me to stay there until I ate it, but one of the boys waiting table felt sorry for me and sneaked it out to the kitchen.

One Sunday morning Mrs. L. came to me and asked what I was doing in the flower garden, I told her I was not there, she said "Don't lie to me," made me hold out my hand, and gave me about four swipes with her stick, then repeated the question. My answer was the same, again I received the same treatment and had the question repeated. I thought, well I might as well lie and tell her I was there and save

---

10   *San Mateo is south of San Franciso on the west side of the Bay, opposite Centerville/Fremont. According to Paul Magel the city was a holiday resort for wealthy San Franciscans, many of whom built mansions there from the late 1860s onward. Orphanages at the time were very large establishments. The Bishop Armitage Church Orphanage in San Mateo in 1886 cared for "orphans, half orphans, destitute and abandoned boys."*

any more lickings, tho I figure she just wanted to let me know she was BOSS and not to be questioned or crossed.

We had not been there long when we were transferred to quite a mansion, with many rooms. It was located not far from San Mateo and had beautiful grounds surrounding it. About 200 yards from the main building was another, tho smaller one, which was undoubt-edly used by the servants, then farther away and a little to the right was a long shed, with an open front and running all the way down was a feeding trough and, if I remember correctly, hitching posts. To say that the people running this were SKUNKS would be putting it mildly, tho I would stake my life that the religious denomination that owned it did not know what was going on.[11]

One day a young woman who had charge of our ward was taking us out for a walk. We happened to pass a dairy where a young steer was tied with a heavy new rope to a strong post in the farm yard. When he saw us he made a rush at us, bellering as he did so, but landed on his back and tried it again. Since he was pretty near the end of the rope it was pretty safe, tho I will never forget how that girl took off, her skirts blowing in the wind, and leaving us behind. One night this same girl in charge of our dormitory was sitting on a bed a few feet from mine came over and gave me a whipping, telling me to shut up and go to sleep. I was crying for my Mother.

One day we were given the job of picking up leaves, trash etc., when we happened to get the school house between us and B. F. Lewaun's office window. We went to playing but finally he showed up around the corner, lined us all up, made us walk by him, and then hit each one a couple of hard swings with his cane. My brother was ahead of me and I hesitated until he was well out of the way, then went by that club in high and he did not even get a good swipe at me. I ex-pected to be called back but he let me go.

---

11   *In late-life correspondence he says that the home was affiliated with the Catholic Church.*

One day an Uncle came to visit us. He brought us each a box or rather a basket of candied fruit and also left us $1.00 each for spending money. We each had two pieces of the candied fruit and one day we were driven into San Mateo and allowed to purchase 10 cents worth of candy each from our dollars.[12]

One thing I have always been grateful for was that two Sisters came out one afternoon and took some of us over into the shade of a little pine tree and taught us to darn. I do not know of what benefit it was to some of them, but it stood me in hand quite a few times in the days that laid ahead.

Another thing I will never forget: a colored man came through the grounds with a sulky drawn by one of the prettiest horses I have ever seen. He was a powerful well-built animal with dark hair and at the time I am certain was the winning pacer of his day. The boy who I was with asked the man if we could pet him and I think he was just as tickled as we were when he allowed us to do so. I can see him smile to this day.

One thing that stands out in my memory was that when we were in England our Aunts taught us to say colf gross lough, etc. When we were first left at this school the kids would say "It made me lough to see the colf walk over the gross, don't cho know," well it did not take us long to take up using the language we had been brought up on. It was at this school that I had my first fight. A kid kicked my brother and I kicked him. We started fighting, and I was fighting away with my eyes closed, when all the boys kept saying to me, "Open your eyes," which I finally did and finally the other boy quit and started crying. To be honest about it I felt sorry for him as practically all the boys were on my side because I was chump enough to keep on fighting with my eyes closed, until they wised me up.

I remember very well while there Corbett and Sullivan had their fight, and I will never forget how surprised all the boys were. This

12   *Alfred Richard had settled in Merced with his family by 1890. The visitor might have been Alfred Richard or Edward Robert, who was in Merced briefly in the autumn of 1892 and for all of 1893. In any case Merced was at least 100 travelling miles from San Mateo.*

is one of the spots in my younger life where I can tie my age into an event that lets me know how old I was at the time *[the fight was on September 7, 1892 which implies that the boys had been in the homes since shortly after their return from London in early 1889, or for more than two years]*.

Living Poor in Merced, Sonora and Sacramento

Finally Dad came and took us away, and we moved onto a ranch outside of Merced, Cal. I remember that it was there I first saw my step-mother. A beautiful woman, tho to say the least, she had no business being a minister's wife from any angle.[13] Those were some days. We were living in a dilapidated, unpainted farm house with a make- shift porch on two sides. My brother and I slept on the floor and the furniture was very much on the absent list.

Our stepmother tried to teach me reading but had me so badly buffalood that she gave it up as a bad job. I remember going to school after it started. It was a little country school taught by a male teacher with a crippled leg who had a four-inch leather sole on one shoe. Tho he never whipped me I saw him whip some older boys, and believe me they were scared to death of him. I saw him make a boy take off his coat, lean over in the aisle, then whip him awful hard over the back.

It was here some big boy taught me to say something that I had no business saying. When my cousin heard me and told me what she would do to me if I said it again, well of course I said it again, tho if she had told me it was bad and approached me in a little different way, I think I would not have said it. Anyway she got me down on a bench and I told her to let me go. She refused, so then I told her I would bite her if she did not, and I bit her and hard. I am under the impression that I drew blood and was in the dog house with all her family, tho my Dad never said a word to me about it.

Later on my Dad bought a horse for my brother and myself. It was quite a cayuse, in fact he finally would get us in the middle of a pool

---

13   *Will never mentions her name. Paul Magel's research shows that she was Alice McTaggart Gardner who Henry J. met during his 1888 visit to London and married on August 1 of that year. From Will's account we can infer that she followed him to California with her mother, a Scotswoman. Paul speculates that one reason Henry J. left the boys so long in the home in San Mateo was to establish his new marriage – one that eventually ended in separation and divorce.*

of water, then lie down. One day I rode him over to see my cousin who was milking. I gave the horse some hay so he would not run off, left the corral and reached down to pick up the post to put against the gate. He backed up a couple of steps and kicked me. My cousin came over and helped me on the horse. I rode over to where my Dad and brother were working, and my brother looked up and asked me what was the matter. I wheeled the cayuse around and rode off, and when I came back Dad looked up and asked me what was the matter and I told him the horse kicked me. He took me in to the doctor in Merced who said my arm was badly sprained.

Later on we moved into Merced, though our Dad would ride out to a farm every day and look after it for one of his brothers who had gone to England to get married.[14] One evening he brought me in a little rabbit that he had caught. It got loose in a bedroom and I crawled under the bed to catch it, well it caught me first right between the finger and the thumb, and I have the scar to this day. A few years before my Father passed away, he said to me one day, "I do not suppose you remember the rabbit I brought you in from the ranch one evening?" I told him I most assuredly did, and it seemed to please him very much. How could I forget the darn thing?

Another time, about 5 pm, my stepmother was walking on my eyebrows for some reason or other. She had a butcher knife in her hand and was brandishing it pretty close to my head, in fact too close, with the result that she nicked me in the right ear. I guess she figured she was going to scare me. When my Dad came home and saw the dried blood on my ear and was told how it happened, I remember he was pretty mad and got after her with quite a calling down.

One time Dad sent me downtown to get something but I forgot what it was, so I looked around and saw some dried apples, which by the way I liked and figured he evidently did so too, so bought 20¢ worth. I gave him them to him and he said, "Why what's this?", and I told

---

14   *This is the only direct evidence we have that the youngest brother, Edwin Robert, bought a farm near Merced during his stay there from December 1892 to March 1894. He probably acquired it in 1893 because by spring 1894 the Rev. Henry J. had moved on once again.*

him it was something I bought for him. Well I can see him to this day, standing there and laughing.

One evening they were having company and Dad sent me with a small demijohn to get some wine. I remember getting the wine, then when I came to where the walk went under some shade trees, the load was getting a little heavy, so I sampled some and it surely tasted good, I guess I must have sampled it some more, because I do not remember anything until I arrived at the foot of the stairs going up to the door. I remember handing the jug to him, then going into the bedroom, where incidentally I was sick. I told my Brother and he told me not to say anything about it, tho the color of the wine was quite evident. But my Dad never said a word to me.

We went to Sonora, Cal. and I started school. This school had readers with stories of adventure, also some with a moral to them which I never forgot. I think they had a good effect on me later in life and chances are I needed the good that I obtained from them. I also remember the druggist's boy who sat across the aisle from me. One day he said to me, I hear that you are poor, I told him we were. It was also here that I had my first encounter with a bumble bee. He caught me under my right eye after traveling in a straight line from his nest where some boys on the school ground had disturbed them. It was also in this town, as I remember, that the city marshal's brother killed a Chinaman and the marshal had to arrest his own brother.

In Sonora my Dad and stepmother separated. I remember we were leaving there and going to Oakland. My Father asked my brother if he would rather drive or go on the train and Alf said he wanted to go on the train. My Father turned to me and wanted to know which way I wanted to go and I told him I wanted to drive with him, and oh how I did enjoy that trip. We slept out a couple of nights. I remember the first night, when we stopped beside the road, there was a colored family living about a quarter of a mile off to one side, and aside from them there was no sign of life except jack rabbits. Some of the land had been fenced in, tho there was absolute no vegetation. At every post there was a jack rabbit. I have never seen the like of it since. Less than a quarter of a mile away there were condors and eagles feasting on some carrion. The second night we camped in the foothills, the next day reaching Oakland.

My Father sent me on an errand to a certain house, and there was my stepmother and her mother whom I had never seen before. She was packing some books, and as it happened she had in her hand a book entitled *The Child's Companion* which had been given to me. I said, "That's mine," but she paid no attention, again I told her that it was mine and I wanted it. Her Mother spoke up and said, "If it's his why don't you give it to him?" so I got my book which I kept until I was about seventy-eight, when I gave it to a little girl.

Later on we stayed at a ranch owned by a family by the name of Haleys out of Centerville, where my Mother died. It was here that I first made acquaintance of their family, tho I should have said we instead of I. They had Chinamen working on this ranch and one day I rounded a building and the eleven or twelve chinks were all sitting down and talking, but when they saw me they casually got busy.

I will never forget one Sunday morning I was out on the porch with the Haleys' daughter Helen, who was about my age. I do not remember what took place but she spat on me so to be accommodating I spat back. She went in and told her Mother that I had spat at her, with the result that her Mother came out and gave me a good calling down. I told her that her daughter Helen spat at me first, but dear little Helen would not do anything like that. I made up my mind that if I ever went back there I would tell her Mother in a nice sort of way, in front of Helen. I did go back somewhere around 1927 to a fire convention at Sacramento, however her daughter had died in childbirth so that wiped the occurrence off the slate.

Finally in 1893 we wound up in Sacramento, broke. I remember how my brother was on one side of Dad holding his hand and myself on the other side and he was walking along with us singing some of his favorite songs, such as "It was there I lost me Kitty Wells," also "Put your shoulder to the wheel is a motto for every man." He evidently obtained a lift from a minister as I remember we finally had hot cakes in a shoddy part of Sacramento. In the place was a fellow in a bright red shirt having something to eat, and pretty well loaded.

He started swearing and Father called his attention to the fact that he had a couple of little boys with him. I will never forget how humiliated the man was and how he apologized.

Father finally helped out at the services at the church of which Rev. Hoffman was the pastor. At last we moved into a great big mansion which had evidently been owned by some rich man who had either died or gone broke. We had the two front rooms and every once in a while the fellow looking after the place would get lit up. You could always tell when that had taken place, as he would come down the sidewalk leaning forward and walking very fast, but I will give him credit, in a dead straight line.

I remember we were there on April Fool's day. Some kids went into a small grocery store, run by a young couple, picked out some candy, then hit for the door hollering April fool. The young couple thought it quite a joke, so I figured I might as well work that gag myself so I went to a little grocery store about three blocks in the opposite direction, run by an old Italian. When I went in, he was talking with another countryman and I picked out a nickel's worth of candy and ran out hollering April Fools. Well I guess the April fool was on me. I hit for the door and glanced over my shoulder and the old fellow was following me, every time I looked back he was still coming, so I went through the gate and left the candy on the fence post. He stopped, took the candy and went back to the store.

Every Wednesday night Father would go to weekly prayer meeting and make us go to bed, well my brother conceived the idea of getting up and playing until he came home. However one night for some reason they never had any prayer meeting and down the sidewalk comes Dad, and altho he did not whip us he gave us a good talking to.

Back to the Midwest, 1893-1898

*W*ill is now nine years old, Alf eleven. Finally we left Sacramento and headed for the World's Fair in Chicago in 1893 *[in May or June, shortly after the Fair opened, since they had been in Sacramento in April and were in Warsaw by summer]*. We put up at a cheap hotel where we had a room on the sixth floor. My brother and myself would go down to the lobby and watch the paddy wagon come down to a saloon next door, back into the curb, go in and round a bunch and take them off to jail. Sometimes they would make two trips, also coming back toward late afternoon and repeating the performance.[15]

One day my Dad gave us enough money to buy a cocoa nut, which we ate. My brother put the cocoa nut shell in the sack and went to the window facing on the alley to throw it out Then he saw a man coming down the alley smoking a pipe, and when he got about under our window my brother tossed the bag down. It hit the fellow's pipe and knocked it out of his mouth. He looked up and saw two kids looking down on him and did he turn loose. We ducked in, pulled the window down and sat there figuring that any minute there would come a knock on the door and we would be in a mess, however nobody showed up so at last we were able to breath easy.

Dad took us out to the fair grounds one day and were we tired that night, so the next day he left us home, gave my brother 50¢, and told him he absolutely was not to go to the fair grounds and rent a boat. Well that is exactly where he took his younger Brother, rented

---

15   *The 1893 Chicago World's Fair celebrated the 400th anniversary of Columbus' first voyage to the Americas. The Gurr family was among the 27 million people who visited it in the six months after the official opening on May 1, 1893. Might the Gurrs have stayed at the cheap hotel established by Dr. Henry Howard Holmes, a serial killer who used his hotel to lure and kill visitors? For an evocative history of the Fair itself and of Dr. Holmes's crimes see Erik Larson,* The Devil in the White City *(New York: Random House, 2003).*

a boat, and we were both rowing along when we ran ker plunk into another boat, and wound up on our backs in the bottom of our boat. We had not seen them and they had not seen us, but were we scared so rowed the boat in and checked out and headed back for the hotel.

Life on the Banks of the Mississippi

We left there and went up to Warsaw, Ill., located near the Mississippi river. *[Warsaw is 300 miles SW of Chicago, opposite Keokuk, Iowa. Its population today is about 1600.]* Warsaw is a rich little town, surrounded by high producing wheat fields, and when we were there it had a plant for making barrels out of hickory. I will never forget how sweet a smell came from this place. Outside of Alaska, this to my thinking was the most colorful spot I ever lived. I also remember that in Warsaw there was an artesian well, flavored heavily with sulpher. At first I could not relish it but later on learned to like it.

It was here I learned to swim by wading out to the log rafts coming down the river, which very often tied up there for the night. It was just about up to my neck when I waded out to the logs, I would climb up onto the logs and dive toward shore, and it seemed ages before I finally was able to get my eyes out of water, to say nothing of being able to get my mouth out so that I could breathe. To this day I have to keep working my feet to stay afloat, tho swimming is now easy for me.[16]

One day when I went down swimming I saw my first houseboat. It was under the shade of some trees along the river bank. I was rude enough to kind of peek in, there was a middle-aged woman sitting on a chair, besides that the only piece of furniture visible was a table, tho no doubt they had a bed in another room. I could not help but wonder what kind of living that would be, at times drifting along with the current and I suppose living principally on a fish diet, tho I suppose with a few potatoes and pretty plain food on the side. What a lazy, drifting life this seemed.

Warsaw was high church. I remember there was a confessional booth just below the altar and to the right, tho that was optional for the members. My brother and myself were altar boys and had the extreme pleasure of getting up to go to six o'clock communion. Dad

---

16   *Local residents in Chelan recall that Will went swimming in Lake Chelan almost daily during the summer, his white bathing cap bobbing along the water.*

always used to get boys interested in sports and one week took the Sunday school boys on a picnic about five miles from Warsaw on the banks of the Mississippi, just above Hamilton, Ill., where we fished and had a good time.

Being the youngest and a preacher's kid I was given the job of going every morning to get milk at an old Negro's house some distance away. I will never forget that on my first visit five dogs came to greet me, two hounds, one Irish setter, an English setter and a red Irish spaniel. They would all come out barking with the exception of the spaniel who was a committee of one, coming out and growling, also showing me what a good set of teeth he had. I noticed they were not false ones. One day I was a little late in going for the milk. As I approached the place there was not a dog in sight and I thought, If I can just open that gate and get inside of that rabbit proof fence I will be safe. To the right of the gate and piled up high was a bunch of fence rails, and I had just slipped my hand inside to trip the latch and you know that friendly old fellow, who evidently had been lying on the other end of those rails, came around and grabbed me by the seat of my pants. He drew blood, and I let out a yell that would have made a Comanche Indian go back to his Illahe and practice up for quite awhile before even thinking of competing along that line.

One Sunday Dad took my brother and myself over to Keokuk, Iowa, where he preached in a colored church. We sang in the choir with the girls. I forget whether I heard any of Dad's sermon or not because I was quite fascinated by the smaller girls. They were immaculately clean, and their skin shone as tho they had been polished with a buffer. We stayed at the colored minister's rectory that night. The sheets, pillow cases and the bedding were as clean as any I have ever seen, and the mattress was pure goose down.

In spring the boys began catching bees without a stinger, taking them to school and tying a thread to one leg. I asked a boy getting himself a bee whether a nearby bee had a stinger, and he said no, so I reached out and grabbed it. . Well I came to the conclusion that bee handling was not in my line anyway, also not to trust anyone too far when it comes to cheap advice. As far as I am concerned that bee is still flying, with my permission.

One morning Dad rowed my brother and myself across the river to where Kelly's Army was gathering at the mouth of the Des Moines river, prior to marching on Washington D.C. This was after Cox and Kelly had split up.[17] I will never forget that sight, there was the most wonderful collection of hoboes gathered together that I have ever seen. I remember Dad asking some of them questions, and to about every one they said, "Ask Kelly." I sometimes wonder if that is where the Fifth Amendment sprung from. There was a big raft or rather scow and a lot of row boats of every description in front of the scow, and I could not help but wonder as to what would happen if they hit a snag on the way down the river. I have no doubt but what if you went up and down the river for quite aways, there would have been quite a demand for row boats after the departure of that scow with its conglomerated cross-section of the U.S. represented by its cargo.

One time in Warsaw I went after school to a boys' house. He was the proud possessor of a goat. He hitched him up to a little wagon, tho there were no shafts, it was just pulled by the traces. The boy had been driving around and decided he wanted a drink so I asked if I could drive while he did. He said I could but he no sooner reached the front door when the darned goat started to turn left. I pulled hard on the right rein but the goat was not to be outdone. About that time I decided I had a little business on the other side of the fence and took off. My timing was poor, the goat's was perfect. I was about half-way up when the goat caught up with me, hooked his horn in my left pants leg, and neatly ripped my pants up to the crotch. So I lost all interest in goat driving, in fact since then my opinion of goats in general has been pretty low.

---

17   *In the early 1890s the United States had its worst recession of the century with un-employment of 12 to 18%. Kelly's Army was a 1894 protest march by 2000 or so unemployed workers led by Californian Charles T. Kelly, who styled himself General Kelly. He marched from the West intending to join Coxey's Army, a larger group organized by populist Jacob Coxey in Massillon, Ohio. Kelly's followers crossed the West by commandeering boxcars but in March 1894 federal troops in Council Bluffs prevented them from using this tactic to cross the Mississippi. At the time of the Gurrs' visit they evidently were planning on crossing the river by boat. Few from Kelly's army were able to join up with Coxey's men as they reached Washington, D.C. in April 1894, so the protestors came to be known as Coxey's Army. Jack London was among those encamped with Kelly's Army at the mouth of the Des Moines River and wrote evocatively about it in his memoirs.*

Another time my brother and myself were invited to spend a week at a Dutch family's farm located half way between Warsaw and Hamilton. You left the main road and went about a quarter of a mile to their farm. It was nice of them to have us, tho I honestly do not remember them ever saying a word. Meal time was very nice, you could eat all you wanted without being disturbed by conversation. I will never forget the man's haircut. His wife evidently put a bowl on his head and cut all around it. There were a couple of girls who lived about a quarter of a mile away at another farm house who would come over every day and we would play "ando I over." Just one thing kind of dampened my good time there and that was their collie dog. He acted as tho he would like to bite me and get better acquainted but I tried very hard not to encourage the idea.

It was also in Warsaw where I had my first experience with fire. My brother filled a student lamp but did not seat the tank correctly, with the result that it overflowed and set fire to the curtains. My brother and I yelled fire and Dad got the lamp out the door before it had done too much damage. After it was over Dad told us to smother an oil fire with a blanket, a lesson which two or three years later in Minnesota came in handy.

I will never forget the wonderful song birds in the yard [*presumably at the rectory*]. There was a walnut tree, a hickory nut, a peach, and a couple of pear trees, which made a home for the song birds. It was here I owned my first kitten and thought a lot of it until it ate my blue jay and incidentally misbehaved in the house, with the result that I lost all respect for cats.

Also in Warsaw I had my first experience with a crazy person and it stood me in good stead later on when I went to work as a federal guard in Juneau, Alaska. One evening a couple of boys who lived across the alley invited me to go down town with them. They had a buckboard so I stood up in back. We were coming home when we rounded a corner where a man and his wife were talking to a woman. One of the boys said, "There is Mrs. Coozie." I asked who she was and they told me a crazy woman just released from the asylum. She had come within a fraction of killing their hired girl with an axe. Just as she looked in our direction one boy shook his fist at her. She looked for a rock in the road then took after us. We only had a block and a half to go to their barn, and got the horse unhitched and in the barn in nothing flat. As she started through the gate at the corner of the house a big woman sitting in a hammock jumped up headed her off.

Later on we went about four blocks over to the street on which Mrs. Coozie lived. The boys were talking to a couple of girls they knew while I was watching the street and alley. It was dusk and when I thought I saw her come out of the alley a half block away I said, "Boys there's Mrs. C. " and one of them said, "No, it's a big black dog." When I was convinced that was the darndest black dog I had ever seen and turned around to get into high, those birds were a good ten feet on their way, well I showed them what running was and by the time I reached the end of the block I had to stop to see where they were. While we were at the corner a German boy came along from her direction and said the Marshall and Mrs. C's husband had her in tow, and that she was talking about killing three boys. We finally hid in the outhouse behind a saloon, pretty quick we heard someone run by and then someone else. We went out and a fellow riding a bike under the arc light told us it was Mrs. C with the Marshal after her. The boys hit for home while I asked him questions about her. As I started on toward home Mrs. C. came out from a lumber yard across the street. I froze, tho if she had seen me I would have shown her was running really was.

There were a couple of rich widows in Warsaw and I do not think Dad would have had any trouble settling down, but I guess that was not in his mind.

The Rev. Gurr was evidently more interested in young women in his congregation than rich widows. In response to a barrage of anony-mous accusations he was removed by the bishop and left Warsaw at the beginning of October 1893. Will was closing in on his 10th birthday. In his first decade he had lived in at least six towns plus London. He and Alf's longest residence during that decade was in the boys home in San Mateo.

Montevideo, "One of the Toughest Little Towns I Was Ever In"

We left Warsaw, Ill for Minnesota, stopping first at St. Paul where my uncle Will Frost ran a drugstore on the corner of Selby and Western. We stayed there a short time then left for Willmar, Minn. where my Mother's Brother, Dr. Edward Spurr Frost practiced, also where my Dad first met my mother, and also where my brother was born. The Frosts had two boys and three girls, tho I did not see anything of the boys, as they must have been away at school. We had a wonderful time there. My uncle in St. Paul had given me a nice little silver watch with gold hands, but it was not very long before I had broken the crystal and the hands.

Dad applied to Bishop Gilbert and was given a pastorate at Montevideo, a round-house town *[a railroad town in west-central Minnesota whose population now is about 5,500].* Montevideo was one of the toughest little towns I was ever in. One night the boys rotten-egged the principal of the school, and Halloween they took the city marshal's outhouse down to Main Street and did some painting on it. We reached Montevideo after the fall term had started. The first morning we showed up at school the boys gathered around us. One would hit you, then when you turned to see who it was you would get pasted from somebody else. Finally we got up against the brick school building where we could watch everyone, however a boy made a date with me for a fight after school. I stuck around but he decided he did not want any of it so stayed in the school room. The second morning a kid from the country shoved me and I shoved back, so we made a date after school. We went onto a vacant lot and fought, finally he said he had to go home to milk so we postponed it for the next night, however the second afternoon I managed to get him with a good hard one on the nose and I will say he had plenty of blood to spare. That cooled him off and was my last trouble in that town.

My school room had double seats, that is seats occupied by two pupils. One day when I came back from the blackboard, my seat mate, who had a hand on each side of the desk, slid over and bumped me just as I went to sit down with the result that I sat down in the aisle. I could not help but laugh, and the teacher turned around from the board and told me to stay after school. At dismissal she came down and told me to write, "I will behave," 200 times. Later she came down to my desk, asked me if I was going to write that, I told her no, finally she asked me why, and I told her I did not do anything to write it for. She said, "Why didn't you tell me?" and I said, "You did not ask me." She said, "You may go home. "She was a red-headed teacher by the name of Miss Kennedy and I liked her, not because she did not whip me but because she was very likeable and a good teacher. I was always given pieces to speak at exercises. One day I was called upon to speak my piece, well I got up, recited the first verse, got the last verse second, and in fact guess I would still be talking if Miss Kennedy has not told me to take my seat.

It was here that the teacher taught us the hymn with the words to the effect, "Angry words are often spoken," which I have never forgotten. Young as I was, I loved this teacher. She was one of the sweetest teachers I ever had, even if she did make me sit with a girl one afternoon.

I very often wish some of my teachers were still alive and I could have the pleasure of meeting them again, and telling them how much I thought of them. I would not have a bright and shining career to hold up before them, however I would aim to convince them that tho I had kicked life away, yet how much I appreciated their efforts.

Dad had quite a Sunday school class, and one day he took the boys to a lake where a fellow had a sailboat. In the center of this lake was a big flat rock. Dad sailed us out to one end where you could get on it. He took two boys sailing with him and left the rest of us on the rock. There were a couple of Irish boys there that had about as much religion as a rock, but they belonged to the Sunday school for the good time they could get out of it. Dan Webb, the older of these two Brothers, and another boy took the row boat and started out when the wind came up and they started to ship water. The boy that went along knelt down and started to pray, and Dan hollered at him "Bail you _ _ fool, bail!"

My Father was holding services one Sunday at Montevideo, the next at Granite Falls, the following Sunday at Oliver. One spring morning my Brother, a fellow by the name of Severens and myself were out for a walk and happened to be passing a church. The doors were open and inside about ten feet farther there were two green felt swinging doors. We happened to hear the minister preaching, so slipped up to the folding doors and were listening to the sermon, when my brother whispered something to the boy with us. He was a little hard of hearing, forgot where he was and said, "What?" loudly to my brother and we took off. Finally we came back by the church, homeward bound, and a woman stepped out and gave us a heavy dressing down. I told her we did not do it purposely. She looked at me and said, "Did you ever hear of the golden rule, do unto others as you would have them do unto you?" That woman sank a little lower than a snake's hips in my estimation.

One winter's day my Dad asked me if I would go down to Granite Falls and get a sermon he had left there. I told him I would, and asked him if I did whether I could stay out of school the rest of the afternoon and he said I could. There was a train coming back up and I figured if I hurried I might be able to catch it, so I ran practically all the way over and back, jumping on the last step of the train just as it was pulling out. I arrived home, gave Dad his sermon, grabbed my skates and hit for the river. I remember putting my skates on, taking my shinny club out on the ice, and standing talking to two boys. That is all I remember. My brother and another boy ran across me up the river aways, they said I would skate about 50 feet then fall down. They asked me what was the matter and they said I answered, "Nothing." Then they asked where I was going and I said home, but I was headed the wrong way so they made me take hold of a stick and towed me back toward town. When they told me to let go of the stick I turned around and started going up the river, so they took me down, took off my skates and in going through town asked me what a team of horses was, and said I told them I did not know. Well, I woke up in bed about eight that night, my brother was still dressed and I asked him why I was in bed. My Dad came in and said I had a fall on the ice and hit my temple on the right side of my head.

There were quite a number of Norwegian boys here, and I will never forget how they would build ski jumps beside some of the business establishments and practice jumping. Some of them had nothing but barrel staves for skis, but it did not seem to bother them any.

For awhile we ate at a boarding house, then we moved upstairs in a house owned by an elderly couple by the name of Turner. One day my Dad was walking with a magic lantern and in some way spilled some gasoline on the floor. I happened to pass the door and took in the scene, then ran into the bedroom and grabbed a blanket and took it in to him, he took it and smothered the fire.

Across the hall from us were a couple of young men one of whom was a minister, tho I do not know about the other. Anyway we were pulling stunts on one another when I conceived the idea of throwing a glass of water over the transom. Well that ended things, because I happened to catch his shirt with water when he was putting it on, just as he was getting ready to go to church. It was the only one he had that was clean.

I will never forget the winter we lived over a hardware store. It had a steel stairway, all open, and I can hear the wind to this day whistle and moan as it tore through those steps, and oh how cold were the two rooms we lived in. The stove in the place could not begin to keep us warm. This was the coldest winter I ever put in

One spring night when my brother and myself had the measles it snowed about a foot and the next morning we got up, put on our overcoats and went outside for awhile. Evidently we were lucky, as nothing happened to us, tho we never let our Dad know when he came home from holding services at Granite Falls.

One summer we went over to Willmar where my Mother's brother Dr. Frost and his family lived. We had a lovely time in Willmar, and it was more like home to me than any place I ever lived. We had three girl cousins there, and those days were the happiest days of our lives, playing hide and seek, going to Green Lake some times during summer vacation, camping out, going on picnics to Eagle Lake, having sleigh ride parties in the winter, sliding, skating, etc. Days that are forever gone, never to return, but which will always live in the pleasant memories of my life, a gleam of sunshine, a twinkling star peering through the darker clouds of life, and tho they have all gone over the Great Divide, yet their presence still remains.

A banker who lived across the street from the Frost's home used to get me to hitch up his horse on a Friday afternoon so that he would not lose any time getting to Green Lake, where he had a summer home. Sometimes he would take me with him, and one day coming back he stopped at a farmer's place to look at some cattle. I will never forget the look of that poor farmer, you could see by his expression that it was just about a case of survival with him as to whether he sold the cattle. After we left the banker asked me not to tell anyone he had been there and to this day have kept my word, tho he no doubt has been dead for at least forty years.

Grand Crossing and Dad's Third Marriage

Later on Father left us with the Frosts and went on to Grand Crossing, then a suburb of Chicago. In the fall we started school, but about the fourth of December Dad wrote to my brother, sending him enough money for our fares and a couple of dollars extra. I will never forget my brother bought a book entitled *Ten Years a Cowboy*. I think I would just as soon have had a couple of sandwiches instead.

We reached Grand Crossing a little after midnight, with the wind blowing and snowing. We went to the house next door to the church, but the people said they did not know where the Episcopal minister lived, so we started roaming around. Finally a couple of detectives going off duty came along, stopped and asked what we were doing out that late of night and in that weather. My brother told them we were looking for the residence of the Episcopal minister, so they took us in tow. They kept ringing door bells and at one residence a fellow raised an upstairs window and, talk about your fluent language, that fellow had it and knew how to dispose of it. I could not help but think if he had had the opportunity he would have made a champion mule-skinner, and no mule could have stood his ground when that fellow opened up. Finally we came to a house where the people said they thought the minister lived in back of the church, so back we went and the detectives pounded on the church door and finally Dad showed up, and did he bawl my brother out for not giving more attention to his letter.

Well we lived there a couple of weeks principally on bread, dried fish and milk. I will never forget Christmas eve. We went to another suburb where Dad also held services. I remember them singing "Silent night, Holy night," then after the program was over, they gathered around the stove and one told of not having any flour, another needed wood or coal, some shoes and so it went. I never hear that hymn to this day but what it gives me a depressed feeling.

It was here my Dad met his third wife *[Mabel Lucas, 20 years his junior]* and they were married around the first of Jan. 1897 *[February 15, according to* Stowes Clerical Directory, 1929*]*. We went over to her family's house for dinner. They excused us kids from the table as soon as we were through eating. All of a sudden I jumped, looked behind me and one of her brothers had slipped by my brother and myself and gave both of us a jab with a pin, which I did not appreciate. Pretty quick my brother came out of their bedroom with a couple of those long eight-inch hat pins that they had to have in those days, handed me one, and started after the lad with the other. He crawled under the dining room table and was facing my brother who was on the other side of the table from me, well that left him in a very vulnerable spot and unprotected, so I was not a bit backward about applying about a half inch of that pin, well from there on out everything was quiet on the Potomac. We left in a day or two headed for Buena Vista, Colorado, with her youngest brother who was supposed to be going out there for his health, tho I never did discover anything wrong with it.

When we left Chicago, his father-in-law who had been a Captain in the English army gave my Dad a tall plug hat and a cane. Of all things to give a clergyman going to a cow town out West, well that in my opinion was the limit. My Dad wore it a few times, tho whether he wore it because he wanted to, or so he could tell his father-in-law that he wore it, I will never know, but I surely did want to try my luck with a snow ball at it but feared the cane that Dad received with the hat. However it was not long before he ditched it to my relief.

From Colorado to San Francisco, 1897-98

We had not been in Buena Vista long before we got hold of a burro. We had a couple of fence boards nailed together and had the burro in one corner of the yard. My brother decided he wanted to take a ride so put the bridle on the burro and led him out. Just then however my step-mother's brother took a notion that he wanted a ride and my brother told him that he would give him one as soon as we had ours. That was not in the picture, he wanted his first, but upon being refused he ran into the house. His sister came out and said we should give the boy a ride first, so my brother said all right He cut a couple of willow switches, put the lad on the burro, gave the animal a cut with the switch, and it took off. Coming to the fence rails it simply sailed underneath and raked the lad off onto the ground. Anyway from there on out, things went along pretty smoothly until the lad headed back for Chicago.

We had been in Buena Vista about five months when my Dad bought a house on a corner with quite a large sized yard, with a lovely stream flowing through it. There was a little rustic bridge crossing the creek and Dad built a dam at one end and piled a lot of rocks at the other end, so that we had a nice deep stream two to three feet deep which made quite a nice place for trout to live in.

My school room was on the second floor of the school building. One day an Italian lady came to school and climbed the stairs to sing for us, however she sat down for a few minutes to get her breath, then got up and tried to sing, but had to quit and sit down before she had sung five notes, then finally got up and went down stairs. I could not help but wonder if her heart might not have quit her later on. Buena Vista had an elevation of about 8,200 feet if I remember correctly, which evidently was too high an elevation for her.

Both my close friends in Buena Vista were sons of two mining men who were in partnership and operating mines in Romley, Col., located on the Monarch Pass railroad route. We went up there to spend the 4th of July in 1897 and it was there that I first saw it snow on the 4th of July.

The Gurr Home in Buena Vista, Colorado, 1897-98   HJG

The side of the mountain where the dining and bunk house was had been leveled off, also a space about 35 ft. beyond. On this space we shot our firecrackers. I had lit a No. 4 giant cannon cracker and had thrown it away off. However it did not go off. I said to myself, I am not going to take any chances on picking it up, as I heard of casualties from that before, so stood and waited, finally I walked over and picked it up and had just put my foot on the step to go in to the bunk house and was holding it fairly close to my face, when BINGO away it went. We had the room to the right of the door, so I called the boys. They came tearing out, so did the lady cook. She led me into the kitchen and put my hand in vinegar which relieved the pain and later on I was able to see, tho I carried a powder mark or two on my face for years.

The day we moved into the house Dad bought, there was a family across the street who were selling out and going to Alaska. They did not leave the next day but the following one. Dad bought some of their furniture and their brown leghorn chickens. They had a boy about my age, and later on I met him in Alaska.

We were in Buena Vista about a year when my Dad decided to put in an application to be sent to Alaska. We all had to have a physical and upon completion of that he was accepted, so in March we packed up all the furniture and left, stopping in Denver for about three weeks. While we were there the Spanish-American war broke out and I used to ride downtown every day and get the mail, reading the war news on the bulletin board of the *Denver Call*, as I remember the name of the paper. In about three weeks Dad rented a box-car, put our furniture in one half of it and a burro together with my brother in the other half. He decided he was going to take the burro to Alaska. You cannot ship livestock without having an attendant to go along. I think when my brother reached Frisco he was capable of out-braying a burro and had had all the burro he ever wanted.

[In the summer of 1898 Will is almost 15, his brother Alf is 17.] We went by train, stopping off in Salt Lake City. The second day there my stepmother convinced my Dad that I should wear one of two heavy suits of wool underwear that had been given to me. My Dad would not take no for an answer, so I took some of the hotel towels and wrapped them around my body, then proceeded to walk stiff legged with them around Salt Lake all day. That evening my Dad told me I could leave them off.

The next morning Dad took me down to the train and gave me my ticket for Frisco and enough money to get along on for a few days. He also gave me enough to rent an apartment, explaining about what to pay, so when I hit Frisco I put in the morning checking places for rent and finally found something that I thought would be within his means and that would also be satisfactory, and as it turned out they were very pleased with my selection. They arrived about three days later and in the meantime I would eat hamburgers for my meals and use the money which I saved to go to shows and buy candy. One evening coming out of a show I noticed a hardware store across the street so walked over and was looking in the window when a well-dressed fellow stood beside me. There was a revolver on display and he asked me how I would like to have it, I said "Oh not bad" and started to leave when he joined me. He told me how he liked little boys etc., also asked me where I lived, tho I did not tell him the truth. When a policeman came walking down the street I told him I had to go.

Outfitting the *Angelus*

Finally my brother arrived in Frisco with the burro and half car load of furniture, tho it was not long before the burro was disposed of. Then Dad decided to buy a boat and sail it to Alaska. He bought a boat at North Beach from a fellow there and hired a gang who hung about the pier to put her on the ways, giving them five dollars which including taking the r__ off, tho that was no trouble. It took just a couple minutes time to kick the timbers out at high tide.

There were three fellows of this gang of about twenty that had been to San Quentin twice, the two Brady Brothers and Jack Cassidy, and quite a few others also had criminal records. Every once in awhile they would congregate down on the beach, go out and catch a couple five gallon cans of crabs, cook them over a beach fire, chip in and buy a gallon of what they called dago red, get lit up and sometimes wind up in a pretty serious fight.

The schooner, which Dad named the *Angelus*, was about 38 feet long, broad beamed, with a center board. She was a very seaworthy boat, if she had not been I would not be here today. After she was on the ways my Brother and myself went to work taking out all the old caulking and putty, scraping the hull, and oiling the seams. Then Dad hired a professional caulker for a day to show us how to caulk, and when that was done we reputtied the seams and painted the hull. In the meantime Dad was taking a course in navigation so as to get his bearings at sea.

My Dad and stepmother had rented rooms up on Nob Hill while my brother and myself slept on the boat. My cousin Ted, who at that time was helping us, washed a pair of striped pants out and hung them on the rigging. During the night my brother and myself both woke up with the boat vibrating. He yelled out, "Who's there?" and a fellow jumped off the planking and ran under the Trenton boathouse amongst the piles. Another night we had three anchors chained together right under the bow of the boat. The gang packed them off and we never heard a sound, altho the beach was gravely.

Dad sent me to the police station to report the theft. The next morning I had to go up on Nob Hill to see my Dad about something. On the way up one of the men that sometimes hung out around the beach was across the street going down to his job. He looked up and down the street, then called over and said to look under Jack Cassidy's boat and we would find our anchors, but to never tell anyone he told me. I kept the request, not even telling my Dad who it was that told me. We started that morning dragging the bay, all day gradually getting closer to the boats, then about five thirty starting dragging around under the boats and sure enough we hooked onto our anchors.

While the boat was in dry dock, my stepmother talked my Dad into making a storage box for food parallel to the center board and putting a lock on it. One day they went up to town, six o'clock showed up and no supper, and my Brother, who could get on the war path if he had to wait very long for his meal, used a screwdriver to take the hinges off and had something to eat. I will never forget how mad my stepmother was when they arrived. She wanted to know what good that padlock was if he took it off, however he stood his ground, and said if he was going to work he was going to eat and she had not come home to fix supper.

When it came time to take the boat off the ways the gang wanted another five dollars, but they did not get it, we simply pulled the blocking ourselves and then tied up for a short time at the end of the dock. Dad borrowed a Whitehall boat *[a rowboat of a design widely used in harbors of the era]* from the fellow that ran the boathouse and one night when there was a pretty stiff breeze blowing, it cut our stern line and it so happened that our schooner caught the Whitehall boat between us and the piles and broke two or three ribs and caved a plank in, so that we had to make a steaming box and steam some ribs and a plank to reproduce the original.

Later on when Dad was working in the boathouse, he either accidently or purposely - I do not know which - discharged a .38 through the boathouse floor when there were four or five of the gang sitting on the beach After that we had no more trouble.

One day I had been up town and came down to take the rowboat out to the schooner, which by then was anchored off the dock. I noticed a policeman standing on the dock and behind the Brady sloop was a rowboat and a big, long-square timber. As I rowed by one of the four fellows inside called out and told me if the cop wanted my boat, not to let him have it, but he did not seem to be interested. Some of the gang had gone over to the other side of the bay and right in broad daylight had taken the timber.

Later on we shifted the boat down to the foot of Third Street, where we tied up at Spreckles Sugar dock. One day my brother had been ashore and when he came back evidently did not make the rowboat fast efficiently so dove in after it. That was very nearly the finish of my brother, as a very slight breeze helped to drift the rowboat and by the time he reached it he was too tired to climb in. I cut the schooner loose and went to his aid, and in returning to the dock was lucky enough not to do any damage to the schooner.

Every Sunday evening my Dad and his wife, including my brother, went to Sunday evening services at a mission church located not far from the foot of Third Street. One Sunday evening on the way Dad encountered a drunken fellow and talked him into going to church, and of course my brother had to take him in tow. The fellow fell asleep and just about the time Dad was in the middle of his sermon the fellow woke up and relieved himself of a big mouth full of tobacco juice. He hit the back of the solid pew and Alf said you could hear it all over the church. Well that ended any more pickups for the balance of the time we were there. Someone had to stay with the boat and I always managed to wiggle that job.

Schooner *Angelus* Missing at Sea

After the boat had a complete overhaul, including new rigging, and sails, we pulled out of the Golden Gate headed for Alaska about the first of September, when the equinoxal storms were due to start. On board were my Dad, Brother, stepmother, cousin Ted and myself. We ran into rough weather from the start and in about a week put back into Frisco. My stepmother had been sick from the time we sailed through the Gold Gate until we got back so she went back to Chicago, where later on she had her first baby.[18]

On the next try, one night about eight o'clock we were tacking in a brisk N.W. wind when a squall struck us, snapping the bobstay under the bow sprit, tearing the bow sprit loose and blowing away the flying jib. Again we put back thro the Golden Gate and had things repaired, also getting fresh water. As we were pulling out for the third time my cousin figured he had had all he wanted of that and I cannot blame him.

I figured Dad would ask my brother and me if we were willing to try it again and told my brother so. We talked it over and figured there was so much invested in the expedition that we would tell him we would try it again. Sure enough he asked and we told him we would give it another try, tho to be honest about it I figured it would be only a matter of time before we would get drowned.

On the third try we were tacking and making pretty good headway for a few days when a heavy storm came along with the result that we drifted south for about three days with a storm anchor. One could see the big ocean liners shove their noses up into the sky then gradually start toppling over into the next trough while pivoting on the crest of those mountainous waves. With everything hanging in the air with the exception of the midship section, you could not help

---

18   *Cousin Ted was Edwin, the third son of Henry J.'s oldest brother Alfred Richard, who came up from Merced to help outfit and sail on the schooner. Ted was 22 years old in the fall of 1898. Mabel was pregnant with Eileen, the first of their five children.*

but wonder how they ever kept them from breaking in two. Then down they would go out of sight and it would seem like the longest time before you would see their bow show up again, pointed toward the heavens, before the ship toppled over into the next down-hill glide.

At last the wind and waves started to go down and when it had moderated a lot, whales and sharks from every degree of the compass came up to get fresh air. I used to like to swim in the ocean but lost all interest in it after that. As we neared the Farallon Islands again Dad left me on watch, showing me the compass point to keep the boat on. I had a wonderful breeze and was making good head way tacking when it was my time to go off duty, so called him. I remember waking up later and hearing the boom as it swung back and forth as each wave hit us and it was not long after when Dad called us to get up and help furl the sails. The ocean eventually became as calm and placid as was possible.

Later on the keeper of the lighthouse together with his helper and son rowed out from the islands, hooked onto us with a sixteen foot skiff and towed us into a harbor on the island where we stayed for a week, with not a breath of wind to disturb the surface of the ocean,. Then a slight breeze came along and a couple of Italians fishing smacks came out from Frisco, and did one of the men walk all over Dad. I can see and hear him to this day. He told Dad that he had absolutely no business taking us out on a voyage like that especially at that time of the year, that he was simply taking us out to drown. I will admit that I did not think we would ever pull through on it, but on the other hand it was a gamble, and so is life.

If you go to the *San Francisco Examiner* of the dates between about Sept 12 and the 15, 1898, you will see where the schooner *Angelus* was reported missing. Well we finally headed back for the Golden Gate and Frisco and sailed the *Angelus* around to the Spreckles dock at the foot of Third Street. Dad left the boat in charge of the Irish-man who looked after the dock, with all the provisions on her, and as far as I know it was a total loss. I do not think Dad derived one penny from it and how much he cost the missionary branch of the Episcopal church, I will never know.

Will told me that after the Angelus *was abandoned his Dad went to the bishop of San Francisco, who was responsible for the missionary district of Alaska, for an advance – evidently not the first one – for steamship passage. The Bishop sent his assistant along to make sure that the money was indeed used for tickets.*

To Skagway

We took passage on the steamer *Walla Walla* for Seattle around the first part of October, 1898. Dad went first class, my brother and myself went steerage. The *Walla Walla* was an imposing boat, if I remember correctly a three-decker, however some years later when she was sailing from Frisco to Seattle, evidently with no cargo for ballast, she capsized, drowning quite a few people.

On our voyage she had a full cargo, also a full passenger list, both first class and steerage. In steerage there was a double row of bunks four foot high, which ran down the bulkhead, then an aisle five feet, then the same number of bunks on the porthole side. When we hit the bar outside Golden Gate there was a fair swell rolling in, with the result that a majority of the passenger became sick, and although each bunk had a vomit can attached to the iron bed, a lot of men never used them, simply put their head over the edge of the bunk and let go. As a result there was a stream of vomit running down each aisle which gathered at the bulkhead and I would hate to say how deep it was. How my brother and myself kept from being sick is beyond me, as they could not open any ports and the companion way was closed. When we finally got beyond the bar and hit smaller waves, they opened up the companion way. My brother and myself decided we would go on deck where we went up forward as far as we could get and sat in the protection of the bow which extended up about four feet from the deck. I think that brought home to me what a blessing, gift and privilege it is to be able to enjoy the wonderful fresh air.

Opposite: Steamship "Flyer" in Seattle, ca. 1900. This photo likely was taken by Rev Gurr on one of his layovers in Seattle en route to or from Alaska. The "Flyer," built in 1892, was the fastest of the Mosquito Fleet boats that served the Puget Sound cities. The Alaska steamers that sailed from the same docks were larger, with higher superstructures, greater beam, and deeper hulls.

HJG

We arrived in Seattle where we stopped at the old Seattle Hotel, long ago torn down. We stayed there for a few days and then took the *Cottage City* for Skagway. Tho we went steerage again we did not run into the experience that we had on the *Walla Walla.* The *Cottage City* was captained by Captain Wallace, a gruff old sea dog but a wonderful navigator. He plied the S.E. coast before it was furnished with light houses like it is today, but never had an accident.

There were all kinds of characters going north and it was the first time I had ever seen a person who I figured was the user of dope. He was a young fellow, immaculately dressed, tho his hands were a lot softer than most women's hands and his skin was pasty white. Later on in Alaska I was to see this fellow again.

We arrived at Skagway about eight o'clock, the first part of October. When we reached the end of the Pacific Coast Steamship Co. dock, here was a fellow who called himself Keller the Money King, whom we had met in Frisco when getting ready to sail for Alaska. There he had conducted an auction near the City Hall and Dad had bought some things to take with us. Here he was holding an auction from a built-up platform about twenty feet square, with an arc light at each corner. Dad bought three knives from him, one for each of us, and we proceeded up the main street into Skagway.

At the city limits of Skagway the red light district was located right up to the sidewalk, with the women sitting in their places in an enticing manner, perhaps enticing to some, obnoxious to others. I remember very well how a corner building might be occupied by a saloon, doors wide open, with the girls dancing and rustling drinks, trade, etc.

I forget where we stayed at first, however in a few days Dad through a couple of lads he had known in Centerville, Cal., where my Mother died, procured the use of a lovely log cabin. I had my fifteenth birthday when we were staying at that cabin. Dad bought some wonderful venison chops and also made a suet pudding for my birthday.

In the short time we were in Skagway one of the boys that Dad knew in California, was picked up for a shortage of funds at the company he worked for, also a postal clerk was arrested for a shortage of post office money. Life was evidently too fast for them.

There was an Episcopal minister in Skagway by the name of Campbell, a short stocky Scotsman, who had been in charge of the parish. Bishop Rowe had sent a man by the name of Woodin to relieve him, however Campbell would not be relieved. One day he took Woodin into the vestry where he had a couple of six shooters hanging on the wall. Pointing to them he said to Woodin, "Do you see those?" Woodin said, yes, and Campbell said words to the effect that if Woodin didn't get out of there he would use them on him. Another story I heard Woodin tell Dad was that Woodin was calling on the people who operated the Skagway Water Works when Campbell came up to visit also. Upon seeing Woodin there he said to the lady, "If you have no objection, I will throw this fellow out" and immediately started to take off his coat However Woodin decided he had another engagement some other place. Campbell's cabin was about 150 feet from the log cabin where we were living. One day I happened to look out the window and Campbell was doing some improvements to his place and reached down to pick up a board, when I turned away. About 15 minutes later he fell over dead, apparently from a heart attack.

Mrs. Pullen was a woman who went to Alaska with, I think, three boys. She started out on her own with practically no money, opened up an eating place, educated her three boys, and did lots of good on the side. We were invited there for dinner one day, tho I do not remember meeting the boys.

Over the White Pass by Pack Train

My Dad was to have met Bishop Rowe in Skagway, but Dad had fooled away so much time *[on the journey north]* that Bishop Rowe had to leave on his regular winter trip to the Interior and left word for Dad to wait for him at Skagway, where he would return the first part of January. Dad got the idea of going into Atlin, B. C., coming out in time to meet the bishop in Skagway.

Bishop Rowe, a Canadian, was appointed Alaska's first Missionary Bishop of Alaska in 1895. For most of his 40 years there he travelled to the Episcopal church's far-flung missions by dogsled, covering some 2000 miles each winter. The New York Times *issue of April 16, 1898, carried an urgent appeal from the bishop of Tacoma for assistance for an emergency hospital at Skagway that Bishop Rowe had taken charge of. "The need beggars description," according to Rowe, with men being brought back from the White Pass summit dying from pneumonia and meningitis (Paul Magel).*

The Rev. Henry J. evidently was more interested in gold than in ministering to miners. A rich gold strike was reported from Atlin in August 1898. Atlin, on a long lake of the same name, was due east of Skagway but could be reached only by going over the White Pass to Lake Bennett and then following one of two routes. One was by water, nearly 100 miles on a twisting chain of interconnected lakes that the Rev. Henry J. chose going up. The other was an overland trail that he, and later Will, followed on their way back to Skagway. He may have chosen the longer water route going in because the trail was not passable until after the winter freezeup. Despite the difficulties of getting to Atlin it was far closer to Skagway than the Klondike goldfields some 500 miles farther north.

Miners with pack horses, ca. 1898, probably on the White Pass Trail
WEG album

Dad went up to the foot of White Pass, holding services. My brother
received a letter telling him to get things together and come to White
Pass, so he gathered some things together and we took the train to
the foot of White Pass. I wish to this day that I had an itemized list
of what he took, including cooking utensils etc. I think it would of

done a couple of men for a two weeks camping trip, if they were not too heavy eaters.

There were two trails to the Yukon gold fields. The Chilkoot trail began a few miles NW of Skagway and was the main trail used in 1897 and early 1898. The White Pass trail from Skagway paralleled it to the SE but was only intermittently usable in 1898. Both ended across the passes in Canadian territory at a thriving trail-side settlement at the south end of Lake Bennett. Meanwhile British investors financed the construction of the White Pass and Yukon Railway from Skagway. It followed the White Pass route but was well short of the summit in late fall 1898 and did not reach Bennett until the next summer.[19]

The agent at White Pass took us over and showed us what they called Dead Horse Trail. This trail followed a swampy piece of ground for about a mile or so along a stream of water. You could practically step on the poor dead horses for about a mile or so. The packers would load them to the limit, then when they would bog down in the mud and finally could not get up the packers would take their pack off and distribute it among other horses and their faithful services to the cruelty of men, was at an end for them. I often wonder if they could have but talked, whether they would not have said, Thank God, my troubles are over.

There was a heavy snow storm on the summit and the pack train which was due in at the White Pass station did not get in until about ten that night. I remember the agent said to the head packer, well you won't leave on schedule in the morning and he said yes they would. *[Winter storms in 1898-99 began early and the snowfall was particularly heavy.]*

We were up bright and early in the morning, long before any daylight showed, were on the trail behind the pack horses and packers. It was rough going, as the trail had been covered over that night. Dad had given me a fishing basket filled with junk to carry, which by night felt like it weighed forty pounds. I could have laid down in

19   *See among other sources David Neufeld and Frank Norris,* Chilkoot Trail: Heritage Route to the Klondike *(published for Parks Canada in Whitehorse, Canada, by Lost Moose, he Yukon Publishers, 1996). This book is illustrated with many contemporary photos of the ettlements at both ends of the trails and of the trails themselves.*

the trail and called it quits I was so tired, but kept plodding up and onward.

We camped that night at the end of a stable, and I am sure I will never forget what manure smells like, along with horses that had been unpacked and put in the stable, still steaming, tho it was about zero. We wore moccasins, inside of which we had our socks and a lot of burlap sacking wrapped around our feet to keep them warm, and had snow for a mattress. I also remember getting up with everything frozen. Dad started a fire, tho I do not remember where he obtained wood, unless it was from [containers for] the food that was shipped up to this point to feed the packers and anyone else who had the money to pay for their meals.

This was as far as the pack train went as I remember. The trail was a continuation of what we had been through though the country was a lot flatter. That evening, I think it was, we arrived at Lake Bennett, where we stayed for a few days. While we were here a couple of fellows arrived with ox meat. They had started over the trail with an ox which continually broke through the trail, rolled off of it and died. So the fellows cut it up, brought it to Lake Bennett and sold it. Dad bought a fore quarter, cut off a piece of it and put it on the stove, boiling it for about four hours. We had some of it for supper, well it was a little harder chewing than spruce chewing gum and you could not put your teeth through it. The sinews in it were a good quarter inch thick, and the more you boiled it the more the sinews drew up and the meat curled up with the sinews. We put it on the stove and boiled it all the next day, then tried some of it that evening. It was the worst I have ever seen in the meat line, in fact never realized that a piece of meat could be that tough and gristly.

By Boat to Atlin

We stayed at Lake Bennett for about four days resting up and getting ready for the trip over water. A couple of Irish boys who had come out from the interior, had built a double ended dory with sides about three foot high, which Dad bought for $15.00 and which he fixed a sail for. There were four fellows leaving on Friday noon, and Dad told them we were going to leave Monday morning. They had a lovely round-bottom boat for which, I will have to admit, I envied them..

We left Monday morning as planned, tho I had the misfortune in cutting a piece of frozen board with the knife which Dad had bought of Keeler, the auctioneer, the night before we left. It split and the blade wound up on one side of my thumb, cutting about a quarter of an inch below the nail and parallel to it, with the result that it bled all that night, but finally let up about noon the next day. I still have the scar as a memento of the occasion.

The wind seemed to be in our favor the majority of the time so that we made good use of the sail. The boat also had a good pair of large oars and my brother and I rowed all the time, regardless of wind. However my brother would ask to be relieved from time to time, tho I was foolish enough to refuse to be relieved, with the result that even today my arms and fingers cannot be straightened out as they should be.

The first evening out Dad shot a grouse, buried it feathers and all, built a fire over it, then after some time raked away the gravel and sand and dug out the grouse. On one side it was cooked beautifully, on the other, quite raw, but when we got through with that bird, you would have thought that he had fallen into the hands of some cannibals, well maybe it did.

During the full week that we were on the trip, we never saw a human being, with the exception of Taku Jack, from whom Dad bought a pound of moose meat for $1.00.

At the entrance to the bay from which we had to portage our boat over to Lake Atlin, an island right in front of the mouth made it a little difficult to spot. However we were lucky in finding it, tho the map we had showed the portage we had to use to get the boat to Lake Atlin was on the left hand side of the bay, when in reality it was on the right side. We could hear a river across the bay, but never dreamed that it was where we should be, with the result that we rowed all around the balance of the bay, finally coming to the river we had heard the night before. When we arrived at Atlin we found out that we had portaged the boat over on Sunday.

About the third night after having left Lake Bennett camp we reached what was called "Little Windy," and the only way they might have improved on the name was to have called it "Big Windy." The water widened out some at this place, and at the far end another bay entered. I was told later on there was a very rich silver mine located there. As we proceeded along this stretch of water the wind was blowing some and to be honest about it the place did not look good to me, however it was dark and we had to make camp, so pulled our boat up on the beach, tied it securely, cooked our supper and made our bed on a Yukon sled, which we carried in the boat, with about half of the sled sticking out the bow. As the three of us slept on that sled, when I turned over the other two had to turn also. I was a pretty slender kid, with the result that my side would slip down between the slats on the sled, my circulation would get shut off and how it hurt. I would have preferred sleeping on the snow. I have gone to bed wet and got up still wet and cold, but that night had anything faded away as far as a night's repose was concerned. It was here, along the water's edge, that I saw the biggest bear tracks along the waters' edge that I have ever seen. I could not help but think of their feet covering the distance across a good-sized old-style dish-washing pan.

That night the wind came up so strong you would hear it way up on the mountain, then it would come tearing down through the treetops, sounding like a cannon ball. It was the first time I had ever heard anything like it, and only twice since, once in Alaska and another time when I was camped at Hart Lake, located in the mountains about 17 miles above Lucerne, on Lake Chelan. When we broke camp the next morning the wind had gone down, but on

Alf and Will in a coastal forest, likely taken after their 1898 arrival in Skagway. This is the only surviving photo of Will during his early years in Alaska.   *HJG*

the beach a little ways from our camping spot were three different boats which had been blown there sometime during storms. I wondered if the bears might show up during the night, tho perhaps they had hibernated, or if there were any still out, the wind might have made them take cover.

The day after we arrived at Atlin, B. C. the fellows who had left the camp at Lake Bennett arrived, and were they surprised to see us. One of them said, "I thought you were not going to leave until the coming Monday," and when we told them that was when we left, they could not get over their surprise.

Dad decided he would build a log cabin, which we did, on Ninth and Discovery. My brother and myself had the extreme pleasure of cutting trees down, trimming off the limbs and snaking them out on the Yukon sled to where the cabin was being built. There we would help Dad roll them up a couple of logs, where they would be placed on top of the preceding ones. That was very pleasant pastime, chopping down a tree, having the snow from the branches come drifting down in a very sociable way, making a snow man, or I should say a snow boy out of you.

After we finished the cabin, Dad decided to go up to McGinnis or McGinty Creek, up Lake Atlin on the opposite shore. Lake Atlin is I think about 100 miles long, also pretty straight, so that when the wind gets a little out of sorts, it can kick up a pretty good swell in a short length of time. Well the wind came up and we were sailing along with a pretty stiff wind blowing and a good swell rolling. In the stern of the boat Dad had 6 or 7 strands of wire which passed through the stern of the boat, then loosely over the sweep. Dad had been working hard to keep the sweep in the water when we came up on a wave but the wire broke and we started to swing broadside. My brother who was holding the main sail, hollered at Dad and wanted to know if he should keep the sail up, and Dad said yes, but I let out a yell, "NO" so my brother released the sheet. The boat had about three feet of freeboard which I was grateful for, tho I hate to think of what would have happened if my brother had not taken my advice. With a square sail and broadside in those swells it would have been curtains for the Gurr tribe.

Will Holds Down the Cabin in Atlin, Winter 1898-99

When we arrived back at Atlin in a few days, Dad decided he had better come out and be in Skagway when Bishop Rowe returned there. He asked my brother if he wanted to stay or come out and he said he wanted to come out and get a square meal. He asked me what I wanted to do and I said, stay there, so he and my brother went out to Skagway and I held down the cabin.

Just a few days before Dad and my brother left he traded the druggist that forequarter of ox for some candles and drugs. Later on I went down to purchase a few candles and noticed the forequarter tied to a rope and hoisted up on a pole alongside the store. I asked the druggist, "How was that meat Dad traded you?" and he replied, "Oh the __ __ stuff." That was all he said but that was plenty.

I remember going along the lakeshore one day and came across the remains of a boat that had been sawed right down the middle. Upon inquiry I found out that it belonged to a fellow called Shot-gun Smith and someone else whom I did not meet. They were partners, got into a row, and neither one would sell out to the other so they sawed her down the middle. Shot-gun Smith carried a shot gun with him all the time and also slept out all winter in the open, never having a tent. I ran across his bed one day when I was out hunting. His head was under a windfall, the bed right out in the open, tho he had lots of covers and a canvas covering the bed.

While batching in Atlin I went about nine miles up on *[the lake steamer] Discovery* and stayed for about two weeks with a fellow by the name of Jim McKinnon. Xmas we were invited over to a fellow's cabin for the evening. That evening he passed around a box of cigars with a picture, if I remember correctly, of Abraham Lincoln on the box. They were called rail splitters and were of the variety that you should be able to grab fifty for a nickel, but if you did get fifty you were cheated anyway. Everyone took one including myself. It was my first cigar. The windows were all closed as it was about zero outside. We lit up tho I just kept mine alight and no more, finally one of the fellows looked over my way and started to kid me about not smoking mine, but I held mine up and showed it to them. I got away with it and later dropped it on the floor where I nudged it down a knothole with my boot. About a week later Jim McKinnon decided to go down to Atlin for a fancy New Years but I told him I would stay at his cabin. After he left I got the bright idea of cutting off some T&B plug tobacco and filling up his pipe. I lit it but did not take over two puffs when the world looked a little different to me. I grabbed a can, went over to the bunk, laid down and managed to get to sleep before becoming sick. When he came home there was his pipe on the table and the can alongside the bunk. He never said a word tho a dead man could see what had taken place.

Those were the great days. I lived on evaporated potatoes which had partly soured before they were dried, Lion coffee (none worse), flour, beans, salt pork, and baking powder biscuits, but had no sugar, milk, tea, or butter. Later I traded a .38 I had for an old 45-70 and some rice.

There was a fellow in Atlin they called Nova Scotia Jack, who was drunk about 11/10ths of the time, and every time he would meet me on the trail he would give the Americans particular hell. I used to side with him and got quite a bang out of meeting him. He figured I was Canadian or English because Dad had sideburns in those days. I do not know what he would of said if he had found out that I was born in North Dakota.

That winter they passed the Alien Law, with the result that all Americans pulled out for the states. I met an old prospector in Atlin, just before leaving, whose daughters I knew in Buena Vista, Col. where we went to school together. We pulled out of Atlin with a Yukon sled, bedding and enough grub to reach Skagway with. The first night, if I remember correctly, we stopped at what they called the "Tepe" where they charged us a dollar for sleeping but let us cook our breakfast on the range. In the morning we were the first ones up, also the first to hit the trail. It was snowing, and after a while we came across 20 head of horses beside the trail. Their owner had dug down in the snow deep enough so that the winter wind and snow would blow over them. Tho the snow would hit them yet they were sheltered and you might say each on had his own box stall, tho it was an open-air affair.

Later on we got out on the barren wastes where there were no more trees, and still snowing, so that we had hard time picking up the trail. Then we came upon a Yukon sled piled high with provisions and with a gee pole stuck in the snow. We took the pole and made out better. Later on two fellows traveling light caught up with us but made no attempt to go ahead, finally we handed them the pole and told them to hunt trail for a while, which they did. At last we made the "Halfway House," where we stopped for the night. Two dog teams that had put up at the "Tepe" the night before finally arrived, one about an hour behind the other. The last fellow tied up his dogs, went in, rented a bed and rolled in, boots and all. I guess he was lucky to make it. We left the next morning before he got up so that was the last we saw of him. If I remember correctly we made Skagway that night and that was the last time I ever saw or heard of the man I came out with.

Working Odd Jobs in Skagway and Juneau 1899-1900

When I reached Skagway, my brother was batching in a cabin facing up White Pass so we batched together. *[Will is 15 now.]* When the wind and snow would come down the river from the Pass, it would very often blow the cabin door open and the snow would be strung along the floor the length of the cabin. It was nothing but a shack made of 1x12 boards, with paper tacked over the cracks, but we were used to roughing it and thought nothing of it. A couple of sporting girls moved into a house next door to us. They would give my brother 25¢ to go down and get them cigarettes every now and them, or run some other errand. I have heard the old saying that a place looked like a "sporting house in distress," and tho I never saw anything like that yet some mornings those girls looked as though they were a good advertisement for one.

I had been there awhile when I saw an ad in the paper for a bellboy at the Mondamin Hotel, so went down and applied. Mr. Tennant, one of the managers of the hotel, told me their regular bellboy was sick and wanted another until he could be on the job again. I got the job and was told to come to work that afternoon at 4 p.m. When I arrived one of the room numbers on the board dropped down, and as the other bellboy was evidently answering a call, I started up the stairs and was about five steps from the top, when I met the other bellboy coming down. He asked me if I was the new bellboy, and when told him I was he asked my name. He said "Gurr, you're not the Gurr that came to Buena Vista in 1897?" and I told him I was. He said. "Why your Dad bought some of our furniture and our leghorn chickens. We lived diagonally across the street and one house down from you." A couple of years later that boy started using dope and was traveling with the same hophead that had gone up on the *Cottage* when we did. You could see life had been pretty rough on him and he was a confirmed narcotic.

One Sunday evening I was called up to a front room where there were about 14 girls and the other operator of the hotel, who was pretty well loaded. I received orders for a bunch of drinks and got two of them wrong, and did that heel jump all over me. Two of the girls came to my rescue and gave that fellow a wonderful dressing down. They shut him up so nicely that he never said another word, and I will be honest, I could have gone over and put my arm around them and kissed them. I could not help but think that tho they were in a poor business, others should not condemn them. Perhaps they should look down their own path of life, or perhaps check their own actions one way or another. I do not say that this holds good with everyone but some would have hard work justifying their own actions. None of us are perfectly clean in thoughts and actions one way or another.

The Hon. John G. Brady, Governor of Alaska at that time, stayed at the hotel for a couple of days. There was no hot water in the rooms, so he called and asked me to get him a pitcher of hot water. As a tip he presented me with a ten cent piece, the first and last one that I ever saw in Alaska. I looked at the dime and felt like handing it back to him and telling him to keep it for a rainy day, then I thought, You are working for the hotel, so thanked him and put the ten cents in my pocket. When the other boy came back I went to get my pay Mr. Tennant told me he was very well satisfied with my work and was sorry to lose me, which make me feel very good.

Later on that summer I went down to Juneau, where my Dad was Rector and for a while lived with a family by the name of Cobb, who was a lawyer and partner in the firm of Malony & Cobb.

I had not been in Juneau long when Louie Levi, a merchant who had a small business and who catered to the Indian trade mostly, advertised for a boy. I applied and got the job with pay starting at $20.00 a month. (I don't think any other boy was chump enough to take it.) One day I noticed that the cloth straps on the delivery baskets were getting a little weak. I called his attention to them, however nothing was done about it. One Saturday evening a week later, when I had a couple of baskets to deliver, one in front, the other behind, I reached out to open the front door when away went one of the straps. I heard him say "Oh Gott, there goes the profit on a case of eggs."

View of Juneau, ca. 1900   HJG

I had worked there about a month when Ed. Russell of the *Daily Alaska Dispatch* advertised for a boy to learn to set type. I applied. He told me I would have to set type for two weeks for nothing, then when I could set a galley of type in a day he would raise my wages. I never asked for a raise until I could set a galley by noon, then struck him up for a pay boost. He said "Well, Billie times are pretty tough and I do not know whether I can afford it or not" and added he would think it over. After awhile he came back into the office and said, "Well Billie, I'll tell you what I'll do. I will give you a raise, but you will have to go out and collect it!" Well I knew what that meant, he would give me the deadbeats that he couldn't collect from himself. I told him if I didn't earn it right there I didn't want it and to make out my time. Three times after that he asked me to go to work, three times I told him I was going duck hunting, the first two times I had no idea of going, but the third time I intended to go. Something came up and I stayed.

He never bothered me again until one time he went down to the States for about six weeks and had another fellow run the paper. He evidently told the fellow to get me to collect for him, which I did. When he came back he hit me to collect for him. I was going to school then and made the rounds after school. On a Friday I happened to get through and back to the office just as he was locking the door. I gave him the money together with the unpaid ones, which he shoved back in my hand and said, "Go nail these people just as though you had never seen them before," and I said "NO! I don't do business that way." He said, "Oh hell that's all right" and left me.

I had a dandy pair of bob sleds so went coasting all the next day. Ed. Russell lived at the top of the hill where the coasting was good at that time and he and his wife could not help but see me. After supper a friend of mine, Ki Winn, and myself were rounding a corner with the bobs when I ran smack bang into Ed. Russell. He said "Hullo there Billie, where have you been all day," and I said coasting. He said "You're a hell of a collector," and I said I knew it. We walked over to a store and settled up. That was my last experience with him tho later on I set type on another paper in Juneau, I think it was called the *Record Miner*.

Hunting

During these years I spent a lot of time hunting at the Bar about 8 miles above Juneau. *[The Bar is the wooded glacial moraine that fronts the channel in front of the retreating Mendenhall Glacier.]* Get up about five, cook breakfast, take a lunch, pull on a pair of Gold Seal gum boots, then go out and hike all day over the mud flats, lots of times getting back to the club house after dark, but what a life, happy and carefree, enjoying nature to its fullest extent. Alaska has always had a soft spot in my heart, and always will, sometimes I ask myself if I should not have stayed there, or gone back.

I will never forget one time I had been down to the Bar and started home about 1a.m in the morning. It was a beautiful moonlight night with a half moon and some light fluffy clouds floating above in the heavens. Sometimes the clouds would cover part of the mountains in darkness and silhouette them against the heavens. at other times the clouds slipped away to give the moon a chance to bring out the beauty which the mountains hold within their bosom. There was not a breath of air stirring. not a ripple on the water as it flowed serenely on its way toward the ocean. Oh what a beautiful night, one that only nature in all its glory can produce, and one which only Alaska can hold within its arms.

Going from Juneau and evidently headed across to the mainland side was an Indian in his canoe, and although I could not see him yet as he approached he was singing. Tho the words were few, he knew them well. He was singing, "Ise going to marry my smooth-heart, under der Norden sunny skies." Those were the only words I heard from the time he came into hearing distance until he faded away in the quiet of the night, but I could not help but think that a person could ask for no more. A beautiful Alaskan night with nature at rest, and a love song floating over the water, and I thought if the young maiden could only hear the song, how happy she would be.

One time a fellow who stayed at the rectory decided to go down to Sheep Creek ptarmigan hunting. We had to row about four miles and I did the rowing while he sat in the stern and watched for ducks coming along. I happened to notice that he was sitting there with the gun angling across his lap and with both triggers cocked. It looked to me as tho I was not very far from being in line with those barrels. I said to him, "Look out or you will be putting a hole through me," and he answered "Oh no I won't" when just then the gun went off. That was one of two times in my life when I have seen a fellow's jaw drop open. Later on up Sheep Creek the gun went off prematurely again and I bawled him out. He said he did not touch the trigger, I told he had to in order for the gun to discharge. I took it, shot a ptarmigan with it, then gave it back to him. That was the most dangerous gun I have ever seen. Someone had filed the trigger notch so fine that if you breathed on the trigger it was ready to go.

Another time Waldo States, Grover Winn and myself were hunting up Sheep Creek. It was blowing and snowing. We saw a flock of ptarmigan on a ridge not far from us. Waldo had his and Grover's lunch in a sack, took it off and then started to climb out of the gulch and up to the birds. I was higher up on the side of the gulch and was just about ready to shoot, when my feet slipped. I got my balance and was working toward the birds when my feet slipped the second time. After we finally shot, we looked around and a small snow slide that had been the cause of my slipping had stacked up about ten to fifteen feet of snow where their lunch had been. Another time I was hunting by myself down Sheep Creek. I had not left the basin five minutes when I heard the roar of a big snow slide. I went back about three days later and if I had of been about five minutes slow getting out of there I would be present today by my absence. The slide came down about a block farther than I had ever seen it before and you could see places where it ground the snow down to glacial ice. An earlier snow slide had caught up a fellow in this region and I think it was summer before they found him.

One day during my hunting days I went down to the Bar and Sam Butts, a professional duck hunter who at that time was working on some claims in the neighborhood of Mendenhall glacier, was at the Bar waiting for some supplies to arrive. He asked, "Billie do you want me to go out and kill you some ducks?" I said yes. We went out and with ten shells shot twelve ducks. I gave him the rest of my shells and told him to shoot some for himself and I would take them into town and sell them for him. We went out the next day and out of the shells he only shot three ducks. It was blowing and raining pretty hard, so he kept the ducks. I went back to Juneau, stayed there about four days then hit for the Bar again. I had been there about two days when I ran into Tom Knudson, who had a ranch down there. He said, "Billie, Sam Butts gave me a couple of ducks but I never eat them, you can have them if you wish." I thanked him and went over to his place where the ducks were hanging up. I noticed that the flies had just bloated them but since I did not want to hurt Tom's feelings I took the ducks over to the club house where I tied them in the creek which ran by the club house. I knew an Englishman in Juneau who had asked me if I ever had any extra birds to bring him a couple.

That evening, before starting home, I shot a duck and waded out into a rice pond up to my waist for it. When I saw Dad I told him I was going to give the two old ducks to Johnnie Clark, and he wanted to know why. I told him that Mrs. Gurr had given about all the ducks I had brought here last time to a Siwash living close to us. Dad said we would keep them even though I told him I did not want any of it and told him how the flies had bloated them and I had washed them in the creek. He said he would keep them anyway and that I did not have to eat any of them.

Well about six p.m. I came back home and asked my step-mother if supper was ready. She said yes, as she was just taking the ducks out of the oven. She put the roaster with the ducks on the edge of the range and went upstairs to tell Dad supper was ready, instead of calling him in from the foot of the stairs, which was the usual custom. I had a happy thought and switched the middle duck, which was the fresh one I had just shot, to the outside and put the outside duck in the middle. Just then my brother came home and I told him I thought we were getting jobbed. When he sat down at the table

Episcopal Church rectory in Juneau, ca. 1900   HJG

Dad asked a teacher who was staying with us if she would like some duck, she said yes. Dad carved her off the middle duck. My step-mother also received a carving off the center one. Dad asked my brother if he wanted some duck and he said no. My step-mother jumped on him saying if she could eat that duck he had ought to be able to also as he had just as strong a stomach as hers. He replied that if he did not want any duck it was his privilege. By that time I figured I had a fifty-fifty chance of the remaining ducks, and when Dad asked me I said yes. Well as luck would have it I received a carving of the good duck. Pretty quick my step-mother went into the kitchen and turned on the water. I did not notice it, but my brother did and started laughing. Finally the confession came out that the center duck was supposed to be the good one. I sat there and enjoyed duck and later on a young lady came in and I told her all about the duck deal, and she said it serves them right.

Cannery Launches, Ferries and Floats

In1901 I took a job on a gasoline cannery launch plying out of Snettisham Bay [*SSE of Juneau*]. It was just at the start of the salmon run, with the result that I averaged about three hours sleep each night for awhile. Our steadiest run was up Taku, where the Indians were operating nets, and tho they were not supposed to fish within a certain distance of the streams, they did not observe the law very closely. On one trip we picked up 4,500 salmon, mostly all humpies and we were certain that the Indians had to fish at the mouth of the river to get that many in less than 24 hours. During the fish run the cannery broke down and by the time they had it repaired you could smell those salmon a good hundred yards before you reached the cannery. It was what you would call a jerkwater outfit. All were all canned and I never ate any canned salmon after that for a full forty years. That was the last year the cannery ever operated. There was no doubt in my mind but what the inspector caught up with their stuff in Seattle.

There was a fellow named Harris working on a smaller boat, the *Pescadero,* who did towing and other jobs around the cannery. One of his jobs was to take the salmon refuse every Sunday from under the cannery out on the bay where an Indian who went along with him would shovel it off. One Sunday he made fast to the raft, then started the boat engine, with the result that he jammed the boat between the piles. Instead of shutting down his engine he hollered at the Indian to push on the pile. The more he yelled at the Indian, the more the Indian became confused and the madder Harris got. Finally the foreman of the cannery, a big raw-boned Irishman, yelled to Harris, "Shut down your engine, you damned fool." This man Harris had had a good electrical education, but was brainless and every so often he would go overboard.

On one of our trips when hauling salmon we had to make a trip into Juneau and I noticed something in the channel, off the starboard bow and thought it was a deer swimming the channel. On getting closer I saw that it was an eagle that had latched onto a big salmon that was evidently asleep near the surface of the channel. It was too heavy for him to fly with, but he would flap his wings and work toward shore, then stop and rest. I have often wondered how that eagle made out, with the fish to contend with as well as the tides.

On another trip we left Juneau rather late at night headed for the cannery. There was a heavy SouthEaster blowing and by the time we reached Stevens Cove both our side lights had been blown out. A little later on I noticed by the phosphors on a wave headed our way that we were going to meet up with a lot larger wave than the rest and, as it came nearer, I quartered the bow so as to not take in bow on. Nevertheless we received such a heavy jar that a forward window on the port side, one that had a crack in it, shattered into dozens of pieces.

Another time during the fish run we had anchored in Taku Arm to get about four hours sleep. When we woke in the morning we had drifted quite aways. A chunk of ice had hung up on our anchor line and cut it in two, tho the next day we picked up our anchor with at least what was left of the rope attached to it..

The night the Canadian steamer *The Islander* sank we were about three miles away, in Slocum Harbor fast asleep. She went down off the lower end of Douglas Island drowning about eighty some people if my memory serves me correctly.

Finally I quit the cannery, going on to such jobs as working for a plumber cutting two-inch pipe all day with a hand threader,[20] taking

---

20   *In a letter written in February 1970 Will reminiscences about these days a passage that reads like an outtake from his memoirs.* "Jorge son of the Jorjenson Hardware in Juneau had the contract for plumbing...and perhaps building [the Convent in Juneau]...he advertised for a plumber's helper and I applied and was given the job. I was taking Louie Lund's horses up the Silver Bow basin after they had finished their evening meal, then going up in the morning at 4 a.m. and bringing them down, after that I would take care of two or three offices, then had the rest of the day to do nothing. The plumber who was installing the furnace put me at threading 2 inch pipe all alone and all he did was sit in the engine room and smoke cigarettes. I weighed 152 lbs. and in order to cut the pipe I would jump up in the air and come down on the handle, then brace myself and pull the handle over, well I stayed with it for three days then was hit with dysentery so bad that I had to quit. I always hoped he would get calluses where he sat down, so bad that he would never get rid of them."

care of offices, and working as a deckhand on the ferry that plied between Juneau and Douglas. On one night trip it was blowing with a Taku wind coming across the channel and a heavy tide running. As we approached the Douglas float the Captain issued bells to the engineer, Ed McDougall, but received no action. He called out of the pilot house asking me to see what was wrong in the engine room, so I went amidships, looked down in the engine room, and there was the engineer stretched out on a bench, dead to everything that was going on. He had taken a few too many before coming aboard for that trip. The Captain told me to come and take over the wheel while he went down in the engine room and operated the engine. I did not envy my job, I had to pull into the float with a heavy Taku wind and if I did not make the connection the ferry would likely plow into the end of the Douglas dock which extended out beyond the end of the float. It was bad enough to jump off that ferry and make the line fast without having to do any steering, however I happened to make it.

On one occasion they were holding some celebration down on the dock on the 4th of July, with the result that not only the float but the slip going up to the dock were crowded with people. Just as we pulled in the slip broke and a lot of the people were dumped into the channel. We were very busy throwing them life preservers for a short space, tho luckily no one was hurt or drowned.

About two weeks later a Slav at the Treadwell mine died. To bury him over at Juneau they hired a big barge and brought all his friends and the corpse over to the Pacific Coast Steamship float. As they started up the heavily loaded slip all of a sudden one of the big timbers in the slip cracked. If you ever saw a quick parting, it took place there. Just as tho they had been trained, the funeral party separated in the middle of the float, some running up, the other half down. That is no doubt what saved them as the slip held.

Dad's Sloop, "A Floating Coffin"

Shortly after my Dad moved to Juneau, Alaska, he bought a 20-foot sloop, and altho it had a heavy iron shoe running the length of its keel to counter-balance the sail, it had too much sail for Alaskan waters. My brother made one trip in it with the rest of the family and a school teacher who stayed at our house, and when they returned my brother told me never to go out in it, as it shoved the bow-sprit under every wave.

Picnic at Silver Bow Basin, Juneau, ca. 1900. At left, arm raised, is Alf Gurr, at the table directly in front of him is his step-mother Mabel Lucas Gurr   HJG

Later on Dad sold the sloop to a fellow by the name of Anthony, a native son of California, who knew nothing about sailing. He kept after me to go out with him, however I kept standing him off. One Saturday he came to me and said he wanted to go sailing the next day and he would give me $2.50 if I would go along, so I agreed. Besides himself there were a couple of ladies due to go along, two Shaw Brothers, a new arrival in Juneau by the name of Reown and myself. Anthony had the sloop at the Alaska S. S. Co. float, the two ladies lived near the P. C. S. Co.'s float. Anthony had hired a little narrow rowboat with six-foot oars to take along. When he asked who would go over to the other float and get the ladies, Reown spoke up, rubbing his hands together and said, "Oh I will, I am a good rower." Well I won't put down what passed through my mind, but I did think that I would give $2.50 to see the guy tip over, however the ladies were bathing and told us to go on. We were out in the channel when the wind dropped completely out. After awhile I turned the tiller over to Anthony and went forward to tighten the peak and throat halyards and as luck would have it just then a gust of wind hit us and instead of paying out on the sheet and bringing her around in the wind he froze onto the rope, with the result that she tipped over. I slipped down onto the gunnel, then stepped onto the mast and as I looked out along the mast, it and the sail were lying on the water. As I started to climb over onto the hull I glanced back toward the cockpit, and if you had stretched a string along I do not think their noses would have been more than an inch from the string.

As the water rushed into the cockpit it closed one of the cabin doors and in the meantime the weight of the iron shoe brought her back up, and I started to finish what I had just about undertaken when we had tipped over. Reown said, "Oh boys, you are not going to sail her in are you?" and we informed him we were, and just about that time I remembered my wish and I could not help but laughing. Pretty quick he said "Oh boys don't, I'll row her ashore," and all we had was the little pair of 6-foot oars that would not reach water, then later on he said, "Boys, I'll give you two and a half if you will just set me ashore, I don't care where." To cap it all later on he told us that we were all single but he was a married man with two children. Finally we pulled into the Pacific Coast S. S. Co.'s float and tied up prior to bailing out. As he headed up the gangplank Reown turned around and said, "Boys, you're not going out in that thing again are you?" and when we told him we were, he said "Oh don't boys, you are going out in a coffin."

School Days

Prior to 1900 the public school in Juneau had been what you could call a mess, kids would do as they pleased and sometimes would go home when they took the notion, so the school board hired Miss Collison, a teacher who was somewhat rough in handing out discipline. In the fall of 1901 she took over. My partner Wallie,[21] his brother, and another boy about our age started to school. It was not long before she told us we could not play pull-away as it tracked mud into the school room. Then we were requested not to kick a football around, and the last straw came when she forbade any snow-balling of any kind or any description, and by that time we were getting pretty restless. One day the younger boys started to build a snow fort and we began running and jumping over it, when the Mayor's boy went in and told the teacher that the older boys were breaking down their fort, and so we did.

There was a big rock in the back of the school and I suggested that we put up a tin can on it and see who would be the first to knock it off. When recess took up she said to us, "It was not very nice of you boys to break the little boys' fort down," and I could not help but wonder what had come over her, but in the next breath the storm broke. Miss Collison said "All you boys that were snow-balling stand up," My partner and myself were the only ones to stand up and she informed us that we could lose our recess periods for two weeks. Just as she was leaving the room I raised my hand, she said what do you want, I said there was a whole mob out there snow balling. She said what did you say, and I repeated that there was a whole crowd out there snow balling. When she came back into the room with the class, she said, "Did you say that to be smart or not?" I said "No ma'm I did not."

---

21   *Also referred to as Waldo. In a letter written in 1975 Will asks his nephew Father Jack whether he had ever known Waldo States when he lived in Juneau.* "We batched together one year and spent many hours together both in rowboat and also on shore. He told a party one time that I was the only one he liked to be outdoors with."

This affair happened on a Friday. That afternoon after school we went down town, looked up one of the school directors and told him the whole story. He said, "Well I am sure if you go up Monday and explain the situation to her, she will let you off." We told him also how we had been told not to play any games etc. Just before we left him I said, "Well suppose she won't change her decision," and he answered, "Tell her to go to hell." Monday morning, before school took up, my partner and myself walked up to her desk, and she asked if there was anything we wanted. I said "Miss Collison we don't think we deserve this punishment, we did not think that we couldn't even throw at a tin can," and she said, "Well I am under the impression that someone was on the other side of the rock, tho I haven't any idea who it was." I told her we were all on the school side from the rock. Then she said, "If I remember correctly one of the Davis boys was there." So I reminded her that she had previously said she had no idea as to who was there. Well that was like touching a match to a keg of dynamite. Her answer was, "Well you can take your punishment or go, I don't care which." I turned to my partner and said, "Come on, let's go Wallie." We gathered up our books and left, and when we did two other boys also quit.

Sledding and Skating Misadventures

My brother came down from Skagway in the fall of 1899 and decided he wanted to build a bob sled. He took a boy's sled, put a piece of hardwood 2x4 under the sled then ran the king bolt through the board, then down through the sled and the piece of hard wood, which did not leave very much clearance. A fellow by the name of Rafe Levi said he would make a hind sled for him, which he did but put a solid half-round runner on, with the result that it would not

Winter in Juneau: Children sledding. Rev. Gurr's notation, apparently referring to the brewery, reads Juneau's First Church: What Have We Come To?

HJG

Winter in Juneau 1901-02: Street scene   HJG

hold traction as good as the front sled, but it worked pretty good. One noon when I was setting type on the *Daily Alaska Dispatch* my brother came and got John Land, the printer's devil, and myself to take a slide. The bobs would hold eight, but as I had plenty of room I laid down on the bobs to steer. It had rained and then frozen and I knew when we were a block away from the bottom, where we had to turn a corner, that we could never make it. I called to them to drag their feet, however they might as well stuck them up in the air for all the good it did. I went well to the right of the street so as to make as even and gradual turn as possible and had the bobs headed nicely down the street, but the bobs simply slid across the street broad-side. My brother and John both rolled off, I hit the gutter, jumped over the sidewalk and plowed broadside on into a business estab-lishment. Incidentally I split the plank from one end to the other, broke a runner, and they had to haul me up to the foot of the stairs where I was working. My leg had been caught between the bobs and the sidewalk.

Another time about 5.45 Dan Kennedy bumped into me with the bobs and said, "Let's take a ride." I told him we could not as the

Pacific Coast Steam Ship warehouse would be closed. *[Their run evidently ended inside the warehouse door.]* He said no, it was open as he had just come from there. Well we went to the top of the hill and away we went, but when we got down to the warehouse the wharf manager had closed the door and gone home. We plowed into that warehouse door and broke the front sled, by bending the runners around and breaking the wood, but luckily did not get hurt.

One Saturday afternoon we were starting out to go sliding. Ki Winn slid with me the big majority of the time, pushing the bobs off, when who came around the corner but the teacher I had previously had trouble with and the high school music teacher. Ki said, "Come on and take a ride" but they refused, however we had not gone far when we heard them call. They came over and Miss Collison said, "Will you promise not to tip us over?" and I answered, "I have never tipped you over yet have I?" She acknowledged that I had not, so we went up the hill, started down and on this hill the plank street broke from a steep grade to one not so steep, with the result that the sleds had cut a groove in the compact snow where they hit the more moderate slope. I noticed these indentations and thought I would slip the runners into them, thereby not running any danger of slewing, well I did a perfect cut in, but all of a sudden the bobs went up in the air and my passengers including myself were occupying the street. They got up somewhat embarrassed and wanted to know how it happened and I told them I honestly did not know, unless part of the steering rope had slipped off and got under the runner, but I did not do it purposely. Well they talked it over and decided to try it again and the same thing happened. When I looked around Miss Collison, who was a tall woman and wore a coat just about down to her shoe tops, occupied a good part of the road, and between the music teacher, Ki Winn, myself and the bobs, we took up the rest. They left me sitting there laughing, I would have laughed if I had been shot for it. I figured out afterwards what caused it. There was such little clearance between the king bolt and the snow, that when I hit those grooves it took the runners off of the snow.

One winter day instead of going to school some of us boys were down on a pond back of Juneau skating, tho we had no business being there as it was rubber ice. As a skater went along, the ice would wave in back of him. A Russian-Indian boy who was connected with the Greek Orthodox church was skating with us and stopped to roll a cigarette. I heard a yell and turning around saw that he had broken through. I pulled off my coat and called to Ki Winn to give me his coat, told the lad to take it easy, tied the sleeve of my coat to one of Ki's sleeves, laid down on the ice, told Ki to lie down and hang onto my skates, then threw the coat out to the lad. I told him to slip his knee over the edge of the ice, but then it started to give way under me I rolled, tried it again, and finally got him out.

Dangerous Charters on the Launch *FJ*

After Dad sold the sloop he bought a 32-foot launch, which I was told had been built in Seattle and shipped up to Alaska, where they intended using the boat on a mail run. It was the best built boat that I have ever seen, she had oak ribs 2x2.5 inches, set one foot apart and inch and a quarter planking, tho no cabin. However Dad put a cabin on her of inch thick planking and a sail and mast. *[Will kept and used the launch after Rev. Gurr left Juneau. One miniature photo of the launch, reproduced here from one of the Rev. Gurr's albums, has a barely decipherable notation that she was the "FJ." Will never refers to her by name.]*

The launch "FJ" used by Will for charter voyages and hunting trips. The deck cabin build by his father is clearly visible. HJG

When Dad left Alaska, I think it was in 1902, I used the launch to take duck hunting parties every Sunday in the fall, down to the Bar, and hired out for any other trips that came along. One day a couple of fellows hired me for a month. They were trying to locate a fish trap site out at Pleasant Island, in Icy Straits. One afternoon one of them decided he wanted to go up toward Haines and Skagway. We were towing a sealing boat and a pretty stiff breeze came up, finally he had to stay on the stern and take in the slack on the painter as the boat came racing alongside on each wave. Just about dark, when we were just off St. James Bay, the rope broke.

I had to come around in the wind, let him get in the boat, and while he was getting the rope ready I made another swing. Coming alongside I threw him a line to make fast to. He was a pretty badly scared fellow and so was I as we were only about 25 feet from the rocks. He seemed to think that I could and should have not wasted the time coming alongside and up into the wind, tho he never realized if I had hooked onto him going with the wind, with his boat facing into the wind, that I would have turned his boat upside down.

We put into St. James Bay and cooked supper and spent the night there. While we were eating the *Anna T. Barron* from Funter Bay pulled in out of the storm for the night. After supper, when I had finished the dishes, I thought I would row over and see if there was anyone on board that I knew. As I came along side, who poked his head out of the engine room but Harris, who had run the launch called the *Pescadaro* at the cannery at Snettisham Bay. I said "Hullo Harris, where the hell have you been since I saw you last," and he replied that when he quit the cannery he took a saloon outfit into the Kuskokwim country, never doubting for one second but what he would make a killing. When I asked him how he made out he said, "Oh not so good," and I asked him what went sour, and his answer was, "Oh they all charged it."

One winter there were three Geodetic surveyors on Point Hilda, located on the western side of Douglas Island. They were getting low on food so one of them came into Juneau to get food, however a Taku wind came up and he could not get back. Someone sent him around to me, I told him I would make the trip for $25.00 tho he would have to furnish a man to do the steering since I wanted to give my attention to the engine as we were going to hit some pretty dirty water. Where I lived on the waterfront a rock wall had been built up which was about five feet high. The tide was just flush with the top of the wall and I had a little canvas punt that Dad had made, with the bow resting on the wall. I had climbed in it and was sitting in the stern when the fellow he hired to handle the wheel, a fellow by the name of Rafe Levi, who had Captain's papers for S. E. Alaska, came barging in as tho he was getting aboard a steamer. He tripped on a cleat, fell over and hit me, and the punt turned over. Every time I tried to come up I was kicked, so rolled over, swam about three or four feet then came up, grabbed the wall and climbed out. Rafe could not swim although he was only a couple of feet from the wall, however every time he could get his mouth above water he would let out a yell, finally he happened to kick the punt which had filled with water. That gave him enough shove to get his hand on the rock wall. Finally, when I could quit laughing, I asked Rafe what the hell he was yelling for and he said he was just hollering for help. The surveyor had come down to see us off and when I looked up he was standing on the planking alongside the house, laughing so hard that he had one hand in the air bringing it down on one knee which he had slightly raised, the other hand and forearm across his stomach. Well that ended that trip, as it was getting toward dark.

The first part of December a fellow was sent to me who wanted to go up to Taku. *[Taku Inlet is the mouth of the Taku River, some 20 miles south of Juneau.]* He wanted to take enough lumber along to put up a shack, also a fellow to build it. I told him I would take him for $25.00 for the trip and $10.00 a day for each day he kept me there. That was satisfactory so he loaded the lumber in the cabin, hired his man and we pulled out. It was only about a 21 mile run, however there are two dead glaciers at the head of Taku, and when a Taku wind blows, the ice comes down with the wind. We got to Point Bishop, by the Taku Indian village, and the Indians informed us that a couple of fellows in a sealing boat had gone up Taku the day before after camping at Point Bishop for three weeks.

We went over to the Indian village which faced the south to cook our dinner. When we were about half through eating, the wind started to go down, I said to the fellow we had better get over to the boat and head up Taku, however he said there was not that much hurry necessary. Finally we got over to the boat, hoisted anchor and headed out. We were within about a mile and a half from where we wanted to go, when the wind came up again and ahead of it a snow flurry, which left about half inch of snow on the deck and cabin. I went out on the bow, putting on an overcoat, and watched for ice, however we were making practically no head way and it was also getting dark so that it was practically impossible to see any ice on account of the white caps. I suggested to the fellow that we had better head back for Point Bishop, which suggestion was heartily approved. As we rounded Point Bishop I shut the engine off, went on deck and personally put the anchor over board, so as to be sure that the rope did not get caught on one of the flukes.

About midnight we rolled in, then some time during the night I noticed that the boat was pitching pretty heavy. Since I had a good strong anchor, also a new 1 and1/2 inch anchor line so went to sleep again. The wind had switched and was coming from the south, where the wind and waves had a long straight sweep at us. All of a sudden I was awakened again with a heavy crash and thought the boat might have dragged anchor. There was a hatch over the engine which I climbed through and noticed a chunk of ice about 12 to 15 feet in diameter alongside the boat. I piled on deck, hooked my arm around the mast, grabbed the pike pole and shoved the boat and ice apart, then went down the hatch to get my clothes on, when bang, it hit us again. I told the man to pull up the anchor as we had to get out of there, however he could not as the wind and waves were too strong for him, so I told him to gather in the rope as I started the engine and ran up over the anchor. I told the fellow who had hired me that we could head up Taku, but he said we would drown like rats in a trap. I told him we would have a stern wind however he did not want to head that way, so I told him it was either Juneau or Taku, and just then the engine quit. I went to the engine and put my hand down near the fly wheel and there was water there. I went aft, took up the floor boards and the water was just flush with the floor boards so I knew the ice had made us spring a leak.

Juneau waterfront.   *HJG*

I told his hired man to get the sail up as I wanted to see if I could reduce the water enough to take it away from around the engine. He stuck his head in the cabin and told me the lumber was tied on with the main sheet, I told him to hell with the lumber, get that sail up. In the meantime his boss was cussing about the fact that this was his first time on a gasoline boat, they had always told him they were no good and now he knew it, this was his first time and it was going to be his last. I could not convince him that the ice had punched a hole in the hull. He wanted to head for the Indian village and beach her. I replied that the waves and the undertow from them would drown us, that we would never be able to get to shore, and told him to head her off a point that we had to clear before turning toward Juneau. He told me we could never clear the point, but I said we were going to try. I had a six-gun on board and he knew it, otherwise I am afraid I would have lost the boat.

We cleared the point by about fifty or sixty feet. It kept one of us bailing a good part of the time to keep even with the water. When we reached Juneau it was high tide and I sailed her up on the beach in front of the Auk Indian village, then we went ashore. That morning when the tide had gone out I went and looked her over. The hunk of ice had punched a hole in her just at the water line, that is I should say, it had cracked a plank between two of the oak ribs and pushed the plank in just far enough to let enough water in to keep us busy.

More Hunting Adventures

One time during the Xmas holidays my friend Wallie suggested that we go down to the Bar for ptarmigan hunting. Our friend Ed Young said would like to go along. It had been around zero for awhile and tho we did not realize it, slush ice had formed in the channel toward the Bar. We left Juneau after dark and had rowed up the channel about a mile when we realized we could not make it, however Ed would have nothing to do with turning back. He wanted to take the lantern and walk up the Douglas Island shore. We told him that we would break through the cakes of slush ice in crossing a slough but that did not change his ideas, so we gave him the lantern and told him to take the lead. He had not gone more than about 300 yards, when through he went up to his waist. When we got back to the rowboat he stood up and jigged all the way to Juneau to keep from freezing, a wiser and subdued boy.

The following year, after we had quit school, though planning to start to go that fall, we decided that we would go up to Salt Lake, about 20 miles from Juneau and have a deer hunt. You had to go in at high tide and come out at high tide, however when we arrived, there were no ducks there. We were camped back in a cove, however I happened to walk out to the point and noticed that there was a north wind, favorable to sailing back toward the Bar and Juneau. I went back and told Wallie, and he said. "Hell, you're crazy." I said "Go see for yourself then." Pretty quick we broke camp, put the stuff in the boat and headed south. We had not gone far when we noticed a steamer coming up the channel and the water all lit up with phosphorus. We could not quite figure it out so I said perhaps we had better let the sail down. It was only two or three minutes when a SouthEaster accompanied by rain hit us. We rowed from about eight at night, until four o'clock in the morning to get into Auk Bay, rowing over the Portland reef, where I hit rocks on both sides with my oars. Wallie was standing up pushing his oars and could see the break in the rocks by the action of the waves. We had to row around Lena Cove in the dark, our oars hitting on the half-submerged rock which later wrecked one of the Canadian boats. Wallie said he never knew it was there and, as luck would have it, we slipped along side of it, my left oar scraping the rock. It was a good thing that we were four or five feet farther out in the bay. We both had slickers on and it would have been our finish if we had hit that rock. The boat was built for a small inboard and had a six inch keel, and the rock would have tipped her over, but I guess that rock did not have our number.

Another time Wallie and myself decided to go ptarmigan hunting down at the Bar. We slept in Tom Knudson's hay mound, taking off our gum boots and throwing them down on the hay. When we woke up in the morning we had to hobble over to Joe DaFoe's cabin, about 150 yards from the barn to thaw out our boots before we could put them on. When we got down to the Bar there were lots of ducks, however Wallie wanted to go back to Juneau. I kept after him asking why, since we had decided to stay for at least a week. Finally he told me he had a premonition that he was wanted in town. When he arrived home, his Mother had lost her mind and was dead in a week.

Working at the Treadwell Mine

A professional painter by the name of Russell received a contract to paint the roof of the Superintendant's house at the Treadwell mine. *[The Treadwell mine, the largest goldmine in the Alaskan panhandle, was situated on the north end of Douglas Island, across the Gastineau channel from Juneau.]* It was a tall building, with a very steep roof. He asked me if I wanted a job painting, and I told him I did. Well he put me up on that roof with about half the cleats or hooks gone off the little roof ladder which I had to work on. When quitting time came I was nearer a total wreck than I had ever been or ever expected to be again. Another lad and myself went to Russell that evening and told him that was the end of our roof painting so he put us to painting the fence the next day.

One time the Jap waiters at the Treadwell mines went on strike. The chef came over to Juneau to get some boys to wait table until he could get another crew together. A fellow by the name of Jim Kennedy, who had waited table before, said he would go over if I would, so I decided to go. We got there in time for the evening meal. There also was a fellow by the name of Jack McGraw. Some of the fellows told the chef that he was a professional dishwasher, so he got the job. I really believe it was the first time he ever perspired in his life. They had a table about six feet long by about three feet wide, with six-inch side boards around it, you can imagine with fourteen waiters carrying in dishes just as fast as they could what a pile up of dishes there would be. After the big majority of the dishes had been brought in, Jack went outside presumably to the outhouse, however he did not show up again so my roommate and myself went out to see what had become of him. When we stepped outside the kitchen door I noticed his apron over one of the swill barrels and said to my roommate, "He has pulled out." He did not think so, but when we checked more Jack was amongst the missing. About ten days later we went over to Juneau, and on going up the street who did we meet but Jack. I said "Jack what did you quit for?" He answered, "Oh __ __ dishes stacked so damned high you couldn't see over them and still acoming."

Once I was put on the midnight to morning shift. At midnight they served soup. A fellow put his soup plate to one side, I picked it up, just then four or five empties went onto the center of the table. I reached to pick them up and in so doing tilted my plate and some of the soup went on a fellows bald pate, he said "___ ___ why don't you drown a fellow," well I got out of there, and fast.

Another time about five in the morning the two Jap cooks (the cooks who did not quit) were making mush in a couple of five gallon cans. One of them jabbered to the other, threw something in the wood box, looked over toward the other waiter and myself and laughed. I let on as tho nothing had happened and that I had not seen anything. After awhile when they had breakfast all ready to serve they took a break in their quarters. I walked over, looked in the wood box and discovered that they had cooked a mouse in the mush. I told anyone I knew to stay away from the mush but so help me, quite a few of the miners remarked how good the mush was.

Stories from Juneau

One day a fellow by the name of Friend convinced my Dad that he knew where there was a creek on Admiralty Island where gold could be panned so my Dad, brother and myself rowed over there. My brother and myself both figured it was mica, however that mica was worth fifty dollars to my Dad, as he borrowed that amount. Later on, when I was working as guard at the Federal jail, this fellow was brought in and charged with some financial skullduggery. There was also a fellow whom my Dad knew in Centerville and a cook by the name of Brown who convinced Dad that they knew where there was a good claim that could be restaked. I had been ptarmigan hunting up Sheep Creek that day, then came home and about midnight we started out for T Harbor, where the claim was supposed to be. They rowed the boat the first ten miles, then another fellow and myself took over on the last ten. When we arrived at the harbor and went up the mountain the snow was deep. We wallowed around in it all day then started down the mountain, and it was a good thing there was no uphill to the return, as one of the fellows would never have made it. The snow was so deep that they could not see the previous stakes, and I think they lost all interest in mining for quite awhile. One of the fellows and myself agreed to row the boat the first ten miles back, however he fell asleep on the seat before he had taken two dozen strokes. His oars got in my way which brought him to, although he only took a few more strokes before he was dead to the world. This in my opinion was just another starter for not only a soft touch, but a build-up for a pretty good sized dig *[in other words a scam]* but it backfired, like many of them do.

A fellow who was working for a merchandise store, on the grocery wagon, had some groceries to deliver down at the ferry float. He drove to the float landing, then got off the wagon and started backing the horse toward the slip. However he was in front of the horse and when he wanted the horse to stop instead of taking hold of the bridle and calling whoa, he kept pulling on the lines and backed the poor thing into the bay, drowning it.

One Sunday afternoon a Frenchman named Damourette, supposedly a Doctor, went out on the channel with his wife, daughter, mother in-law and a baker. They had a small sail on the boat, however it turned over. The baker, seeing that if someone did not reach shore pretty quick they all would drown, struck out for the Douglass shore, about 150 yards away, while Damourette called out "Dats right, swim for de shore baker, swim for de shore." At the time I was decking on the ferry that plyed between Juneau and Douglas. Damourette went over to Douglas the next morning on the ferry and told of saving his wife, daughter, mother in law, himself and the baker by saying "Swim for de shore baker, swim for de shore."

Juneau in its earlier days had business men who had committed some crime or other in the States and were wanted by the Federal government for murder and on down to lesser offences. There was a fellow in Juneau who said he could of cleaned up a fortune for telling on fellows wanted, however he knew if he ever told on one, some other wanted ones would eliminate him in a hurry. There was a fellow in business there that I always figured I would not want to cross in any way, and later on found out that there was a reward on his head of $5,000 for murder. Another man I was told had served eight years for shooting another man, and did not make any bones about it, also saying he had never met the man he was afraid of yet. Later, on a 4th of July, I was standing within a couple of feet of the man who I think made him change his ideas, and also was I think the cause of the fellow quitting Alaska in less than a year. They were both from Montana and knew each other there. Later on this bad? man was Superintendent at the Sheep Creek mines when Jack Love, the other man, was teaming there. Jack told me that he did not remember how the conversation drifted around that way, however the Supt made the remark that he had never seen the man he was afraid of yet, and Jack told him that there was always a better man than oneself and the Supt said he'd be glad to meet him. Jack told him if he felt that way about it sooner or later he would, and to remember what he told him. Jack Love was the one who changed his ideas.

Six Months in Sitka, 1903[22]

My six months in Sitka began when the painter I had worked for told me that Geo. E. James of Juneau,[23] who had a contract to build a Government coal bunker on Japonsky Island off Sitka, wanted a painter, so I went over on the *Str. Bonita,* on which my partner *[evidently Wallie]* was quartermaster. On the way over I steered part of the time and was offered a job as quartermaster. The Captain in charge was pretty rough and I knew if he bawled me out for his orders that happened to go wrong, I would not be on the job after that.

I arrived at Sitka a little after noon. What a place Sitka was in those days. When I was there in 1903 the town was 106 years old. When Alaska was sold to the U.S. most all of the higher class Russians went back to Russia, with the result that there was some disease scattered about, together with epileptics and what have you, altho there were also some very nice people there. *[Sitka had been capital of Alaska territory since the U.S. purchased it in 1867. By 1903 it was in decline.]*

I had met the fellow who was running the dray at the ferry landing when he had been over to Juneau on jury duty, the first time he had ever been out of Sitka. He told me that if I ever came over to Sitka he would show me the town. Well in those days it was some town. There was a Marine barracks, three saloons, a couple of merchandise stores and a barber shop, the Greek orthodox church, the Episcopal church and an Indian mission run by the Presbyterian church, whose Pastor had formerly been at Juneau. The only thing to break the monotony or disturb the peace were the mission bells at six every evening. If it had not been for my pride I would have climbed back on the boat and gone back to Juneau.

---

22   *The memoirs have multiple and discontinuous versions of Will's time in Sitka, and I have taken more liberties than elsewhere in putting them into a coherent account.*

23   *George E. James was an architect who had designed Holy Trinity Church in Junuea, built in 1896. – Paul Magel*

Instead I climbed on the outfit, had my trunk delivered at Myers Hotel, then set out to see the town. The dray was pulled by a poor old horse that you could just about hang your hat on any place, and a wagon that should have been stored away in a wagon shop's antique section. The only thing worth seeing was Lovers Lane. One Sunday morning I went into Mills Brothers merchandise store as the door was open and a fellow was sweeping out. I bought 50 cents worth of candy, and incidentally asked the fellow how long he had lived there. He scratched his head, did a lot of heavy thinking and said, "Let's see, about 25 years." I looked at him and said, "You were born here weren't you?" And in a very meek voice he said yes. He had been born and raised there, and had never left Sitka.

I used to kid the fellow that drove the dray every time I met him. One day while waiting for the ferry from Juneau to arrive I bumped into him accompanied by a pious Marine (something quite scarce at the time) and was razzing him about Sitka when he said "Oh you needn't talk, going up the streets of Sitka at four o'clock in the morning, hollering hurrah for America." [*The implication was that Will was roaring drunk.*] My partner Wallie heard this and suggested that we all go up and call on the Rev. Bannerman and his wife. I guess that Marine swallowed the story hook, line and sinker, for we were no sooner located comfortably in the front room when the Reverend turned loose with a wonderful lecture against drinking. In fact at that time and for a long time afterwards liquor was not on my menu, not that I might not have drank it if it tasted good to me, but the stuff never appealed to me. However I let the tale stand, never telling the Reverend that the remark was said in jest.

Sitka had a dance hall with a player piano, and amongst the rolls they had were five quadrilles. It was something to behold the rhythm displayed by the dancers on Saturday evenings, most of them Marines and their wives or girls. They had danced them so long that they would go through the quadrilles in perfect time.

When I first arrived in Sitka my work for Geo. E. James did not start for a week or ten days. In the meantime Miss Patton, a sister-in-law of the Governor of Alaska, who also resided at Sitka at that time, looked me up and asked me if I would help out on the Sitka weekly paper which she owned and edited. As I had nothing to do I told her I would. I presume some way or other she found out that I had set type on a couple of the Juneau papers. When I showed up at the office who was putting out the paper for her but a fellow named Schebbler who was mixed up in the Bird murder case that happened up North about 1900. I had very little use for him and hated to associate with him even in a business way. He incidentally wore a bright red tie, a land mark of what he formerly was.[24]

I stayed at the Meyers hotel for two months and it was out of this world. I don't think one brewery alone could have kept Mrs. Meyers supplied with beer. *[Either the hotel had a well-patronized bar or Mrs. Meyers was a drunk, or both].* She put in pretty late hours, with the result that our lunch buckets suffered. One morning I had a small boiled potato in my lunch and one sandwich. I told her I could eat two sandwiches as easily as one and for a couple of days I had two sandwiches, then one cut in two. Then one morning I had an egg that had never seen boiling water, together with a piece of half baked pie that was three-fourths of an inch across the widest part. I took the pie, slammed it down on the bottom of my lunch bucket, then put the egg on top of it, and took it back that night.

Another fellow by the name of Jones and myself had the hotel's back room in the attic with a door opening onto the good fresh air. There was no outside stairway, so if you felt so inclined you could either jump, fall or be pushed out the door. We had not been there very long when one of the waiters and Mrs. Meyers got the idea of doing a little serenading by singing below our door, well I cooled that idea with a glass of water. The next night the other waiter tipped me off that my bed had been loaded with pins. It was not long before the two of us quit the hotel and went to batching.

---

24   *Alaska was relatively lawless from 1867 until 1899, the year that the US Congress enacted the Code of Criminal Procedures for the Territory of Alaska. Before then mining districts and individual camps could set up their own courts to administer justice according to their interpretation of common law. The Bird murder case captured the attention of most Alaskans at the time. Homer Bird shot and his killed his partner in front of several witnesses and was one of the first murderers to be tried by civil authority in Alaska. He was found guilty by a jury and hanged in Sitka in 1903. – Paul Magel*

The Alaska experimental farm was located at Sitka. My friend and myself rented a house adjoining the farm, and noticed that they had string run thro the wheat to help it to stand, the stems were so weak. The woman living in the house we rented had gone crazy, and to be honest about it I did not blame her, I think if I had stayed there very long I would have gone crazy too, or perhaps I was a little unbalanced for staying in the first place.

The deer there were small and you could buy one from the Indians for five or six dollars. We lived on deer meat twice a day for about two months. But how I would like to have some of that deer meat now, it was as tender as any meat could be and what a fine wild flavor.

While I was in Sitka a couple of Russians showed up and went to work for Geo. E. James. Their hands showed no work whatsoever had been done by either one, like the hands of a woman who had servants. The older of the two was so bitter that he could not contain himself and the younger of the two would calm him down. He took a personal dislike to me, I think because I was a friend of the Geo. E. James family and also because my Dad was an Episcopal Minister. They held private meetings nights tho I was never asked to go, however later on I had an invitation to go deer hunting with one of them and his wife whom I had never met. I felt confident that if I went I would never come back. Some years later I saw a picture of Lenine, and he was the vicious one, the other fellow's picture I saw later on in a newspaper with some prominent Russians, tho he had changed a lot. Later on I read an account of Lenine's life, however it did not mention him having been in Alaska. No doubt he covered that over to protect contacts in Sitka. I would stake my life tomorrow that the fellow was Lenine. *[Will remembers this episode through the lens of the Cold War. No doubt he is referring to Vladimir Lenin but Lenin could not have been in Sitka in 1903. In that year he lived a well-documented life in London and Geneva. The Russians probably were political exiles from Czarist Russia. Some political opponents of absolutist rule were held in prison camps in Siberia, others were forced into exile. Many were professionals and intellectuals of privileged backgrounds and returned to St. Petersburg to participate in the constitutional government established in 1905-06. It is unfor-*

tunate that Will did not overcome his suspicions and interact more closely with them.]

As for work on Japonsky Island, I arrived sooner than I was wanted so Geo. James put me to firing a donkey *[engine]*, scrubbing brushes, dipping shingles in creosote and going over to Sitka for things needed, later on painting the new coal bunker and officer's house which he had erected. One day I noticed that the old coal bunker which Geo. James had built and which sat right in front of the new one had the back end bulged out. They had forgotten to anchor the iron bolts which were supposed to fasten the side timbers to the timbers across the rear end, with the result that the coal had pushed the end out some. The collier would come up with about 30,000 tons *[pounds?]* of coal, dumping it in the front of the bunker and continuing toward the back, with the result that nothing but screenings reached the back. Geo. James put a couple of Canadians in there shoveling it out at about the time I was pretty well wound up with my work. When I asked him what next, he told me I could go in and help those boys. I worked all day and that night I could spit coal dust to perfection.

The next day Long Lake was frozen over, and the ice was wonderful, so I put in a couple of days skating. When I went back Geo. James asked me where I had been and I told him skating. The work in my line was just about all wound up, thought he did ask me to go to work on the pile driver crew. But Wallie told me that the man with whom I had left the boat with was running up quite a machine bill on her so I decided to head back to Juneau.

The last night I was in Sitka, I was uptown until about midnight. I had on a new blue serge suit, a pair of Hanon vici kid *[suede]* shoes, a pair of gold cuff links and a new fedora hat. Then I went down to the dock to go aboard the ferry *George* and go to bed. First though I went looking for the restroom, but could not find it so thought I would go over in the shadow of a little warehouse on the dock. To get down on the dock from the land side you had to go through an arch which ran through the center of the warehouse, and at the dock end there was an electric light hanging in the arch. To the left of this as you came down on the dock from the land side was the warehouse, and just beyond this, and in the warehouse's shadow, was the top of a pile driver. They had passed a big hawser over the guard rail, around one of the piles, then back over and tied the rope down so if the wind happened to blow the pile driver over into the channel they would not lose it. I went kicking along with one foot expecting to hit the guard rail, but found myself falling. I knew that at low tide there was a jagged bunch of rocks covered with kelp so bunched my hands and feet in front of me. Luckily there was enough water over them that I did not hit any.

I figured I could hang onto a pile and call to the night watchman on the *Excelsior,* but I could not see which pile the rope was around. I guessed which it might be, knowing if I missed I could climb down and swim to the one with the rope. As luck would have it I hit the right pile, pulled myself over the edge, let the water drain off me some, then casually sauntered out where the electric light hit me. The night watchman stopped in his tracks. He no doubt had heard me hit the water, but had also noticed me walk over in the first place. If his head had been working he would have come over when he heard me hit the channel. I turned around and sauntered back in the shadow of the building. When some more water had drained off me I went up to the federal building, the first building on the right, and dried off, and took off the majority of my clothes and dried them too.

About 1.30 a.m. the deputy U.S. Marshall came by and told the guard not to call him unless it was of a very serious nature. About 2.30 a fellow came running down and said a Russian whose name I now forget had threatened to knife a fellow where they were having a party. The guard was worried so I told him I would go up and look into the matter, but by the time I arrived the party had broken up

My blue suit survived the event though I lost a new fedora hat and ruined a good pair of Hanon vici kid shoes. The second of December, I think it was, I was headed back for Juneau on the *George.*

Back in Juneau

When I was working in Sitka I left the boat with a Juneau photographer by the name of G. Winters. He commended me on using good judgment by picking a person of maturity, also one in business, etc. But my partner, who was quartermaster on the *Bonita,* plying between Juneau and Sitka, told me that Winters was running up quite a repair bill on the engine, so after six months I returned to Juneau. By the time I was through paying for the machine and gas bill, I was broke and had to go and ask a Juneau merchant, Chas. Goldstein, for credit to get some groceries. It was rather humiliating to me to have to ask, but he gave it to me.

About a day after I returned to Juneau while going up the street I met Dan Kennedy. He said "Hullo Billie, where the hell have you been?" I told him I had been over to Sitka for six months. He wanted to know what I was going to do now and I said I thought I would go duck hunting up at the Bar, eight miles above Juneau. He said, "In this kind of weather?" but I said I was going in the launch which had a cook stove and a cabin on it. He said, "Well that would be kind of a pleasure trip wouldn't it?" and I said yes. He asked me who was going with me and I told him no one. He asked what the chances were to go along, I told him fine, then he said he had no gun. I said I would loan him mine as there were three or four people who had told me any time I wanted to borrow a gun to come and get theirs. I went to borrow one from a party and got to his house about 9 p.m. He brought out an old double-barreled shotgun, telling me that there was not another gun like it in the U.S., and that it was made especially for a certain Governor, tho I forgot who he said. He mentioned that the stock was cracked and should be wrapped with copper wire, but still kept on telling me what a good gun it was, then just as I was leaving he said, "You want to be kind of careful, when you pull one trigger the other goes off." When we arrived at the Bar we anchored, then the next morning started looking for ducks and only saw one flock. They were up a slough so I crawled up it to within shooting distance and let go with the only barrel that I loaded, but no ducks stayed put.

On Thursday we decided to head back for Juneau. There was a dance that night at the opera house and Dan had a date to take a girl, so we pulled up anchor at high tide and headed for home. There was a fairly stiff breeze blowing and just as we got up to the narrow section where the tide is pretty strong, the engine quit, so we hoisted the sail and were just through the straits when the throat halyard broke loose from the mast. We went on the beach on the Douglas Island side. Dan got in the row boat, taking the anchor out and heaving it over while I payed out the anchor line. We both got pretty wet and had to stay on the boat until the tide ran out and came in again before we could get off the beach. We had no wood to build a fire and poor old Dan missed his appointment and his dance. Every time Dan would meet me on the street after that he would look at me and say with plenty of disgust, "Pleasure trip, well I'll be ___ ___"

Federal Jail Guard, 1904-1905

The summer of 1904 the capital was moved from Sitka to Juneau *[evidently the jail was moved in 1904, the seat of government not until 1906]*. I was told two or three times that I could have a job as guard if I wanted it, though I was not quite 21. Finally I decided to take it. There were two guards on a shift, which should have stayed that way but Kelly the jailer, who was born and raised in Waterville, thirty-five miles from Chelan, he figured the place could be run by one guard on a shift. He would come up when the food was passed in then come back up when the dishes were taken out, which in my opinion was false economy.

When I first went to work at the jail a fellow by the name of Butler was brought down from Haines. He was bad medicine. I came on shift one evening and noticed that he had shackles on his ankles. At feeding time I made the rounds and he was sitting on his bunk while the other fellows were eating. In about ten minutes I made another round and he had them off, and he told me in very plain language what I could do with them. I stood and talked to him for a few minutes, went on out and when I came back later on he had put them back on and we never had one bit of trouble with him from then, not until his sentence was up. I surely was glad that I had taken the time to talk it over with him, and not report to Kelly what he had first said to me when he had taken them off.

I went on shift at 4 p.m. getting off at midnight. Sometime after I began working there some of the baseball boys came to me one evening and offered 35.00 dollars if I would row up to Auk Bay, a distance of fifteen miles, and tell Judd Baggs, a Juneau pitcher who was camped up there with his lady friend, that they wanted him to row out and meet a northbound steamer to go up to Skagway to play ball. I told them if they would furnish me a good rowboat I would go. I grabbed some lunch, then headed for Auk Bay. When I hit the beach Judd Baggs came down to meet me. I delivered my message and then headed back for the boat. He said "You are not going right back," I told him I was, and he said "Why you haven't had anything to eat," and I replied no, I had not. I cannot forget the look that came over his face, though I do not know whether it was because of respect for my endurance or whether he thought I was about the craziest guy he had ever met.

I figured I could be back in time to stand my shift, however the tide held me up about twenty minutes getting back across the bar, then I hit a headwind and did not get back until after five p.m. The guards that were not working offered to stand my shift, but Kelly the jailer would not let them, and went up and told the U.S. Marshal that I had left and knew I could not get back but had made no arrangements. I was told later that his interpretation did not go over very big with the U.S. Marshal, James M. Shoup. I guess he figured that things had gone wrong some place along the line.

There was an element around Juneau that liked to get picked up in the fall so that they could live through the winter at the expense of the Governor. However one spring day Kelly was down around the water front and picked up a fellow selling a bottle of liquor to an Indian. Well Patty the Pig, as he was nicknamed, did not want to go to jail for the summer, so hired a Negro lawyer who lived down near the waterfront to defend him. Patty paid him five dollars, no doubt the five he got from the Indian for the bottle of hootch. They got into Judge Folsom's court and the colored lawyer said his piece, then Judge Folsom turned to Patty and said, "Well Patty, what have you got to say to defend yourself?" Of course the more that type of fellow talks the more apt he is to hang himself. Patty opened up, and finally Judge Folsom looked down at him and said, "Patty, after listening to the evidence, I cannot help but thing you are guilty." The colored lawyer chimed in and said,"Yes Judge, I think he is guilty too." The next day when I had Patty working on the wheel barrow, he would spit on his hands, grab hold of the wheel barrow and say, "I gave de ___ ___ _ ___ five dollars to trow me down."

One morning, about 2 a.m. Johnnie Snook, the Deputy U.S. Marshal at Skagway, brought in a Salvation Army man. I started to search him and Snook said, "You need not search him, he hasn't anything." I replied, "Those are our orders," and found a roll of about $288.00

fastened around his ankle with a couple of rubber bands. Snook looked at him and said, "I thought you told me you did not have anything." He was a small slender man but had a quick tongue. He looked at the prisoner and said, "Does preaching go with lying?"

I was there about six months when the Marshal called me upstairs and asked me if I cared to come down to the States with prisoners who were to go to McNeils Island, a Jap and two Indians. I stood there figuring on the finances, for although I would have my way paid down and back, and all expenses, I wanted some spending money. Finally I said yes, went down stairs, borrowed 100.00 from one of the guards and borrowed a little more in Seattle. The Marshal told someone I acted as tho I did not know whether I wanted to go or not.

One night when I came on shift at midnight, I noticed that we had received a demented man. He had been in an institution in Colorado twice. When we took the poor fellow up for a hearing, when he got up in the court room he began jumping and stomping, and imagined that he was riding broncos. No doubt he had some time or other been thrown and lit on his head. In the cell I tried to get some dope down him in some coffee. I asked him if he wanted something to drink, he wanted to know if we had any champagne, I told him yes, so went out and got some coffee and put dope in it. He tasted it said that was the damndest champagne he had ever tasted, it was not, and he proceeded to throw the contents through the bars at me. Later on I had to take a couple of trustees in and dress him. He had stripped down, said he was born naked and be __ __ if he wasn't going to stay that way.

We had a locoed chinaman in jail and for the time he was there he was kept on the side with the fellows who had committed murder or some other felony. One night when I went to get the dishes out the chinaman swung around, grabbed the bar and tried to push the gate open.

I hooked onto the bars, held him from getting out, and called Kelly. He came into the corridor, reached over my shoulder and tapped that chinaman on the head with his billie. When that chink shot in toward the center of the room and turned around, rubbing the back of his head as tho it was a kind of serious situation, I wanted to laugh.

I worked at the jail from about June 1904 until January 1st, 1906 and was there longer than any other guard. I also was the only one that had not lost a prisoner, though I was on day shift with Kelly for 11 months straight after my first month. He told a party that I was the only one that did things the way he wanted them done, and when I quit the U.S. Marshal told someone that I was the best guard that he ever had, which made me feel pretty good.

Will Gurr, ca. 1906. Studio portrait by Winter Pond, Juneau. Will has matured greatly during his seven years in Alaska, and can dress very well, as he describes in his account of the six months he spent in Sitka.   *LCHM*

Two Thieves and a Suicide

I figured I wanted more money as I was only getting $75.00 a month as a guard so applied at B.M. Behrends store as they were losing their delivery man but was turned down. A friend later on told me that Ross-Higgins Co., a general merchandise store down on the waterfront, was going to need a man, so went down and applied. I quit the Federal jail Dec. 31st., 1905 and went to work for Ross Higgins and Co. on Jan. 2nd 1906. Later I was told that my age was the only thing that kept me from getting the Deputy U.S. Marshall's job at Skagway, when Johnnie Snook quit and went down to Idaho to take charge of the State penitentiary.

One day the head grocery man told me he was convinced a couple of women were stealing but he could never catch them. He said he thought they took turns, one stealing one time, the other the next. I told him they would not be hard to catch, so we proceeded to get lined out. In the back of the store was a stairway going up to a balcony with a railing across it. We ran some muslin thro the rails. The next time they came in that was the first thing they noticed, but we told them it was such an unsightly view from the front of the store that we decided to make it look neater. The manager of the store had told us if we ever caught them to tell them we did not want their business any more. It was about a month before they came in and I happened to be in from deliveries, so I went upstairs and hid. We tripped them up, but that store was catering to their business in a week. They made a perfect chump of the head grocery man and I finally stepped in and told them off. But that ended my helping catch or prevent any more things along that line.

I had been working for this firm for about 60 days when I had my wages raised. One day the manager, Mr. Gordes, came to me and said, "Will I understand you are quitting us." I told him that later on, toward the first of the year, I figured on going South. I said I would give him thirty days' notice and if that was not enough I would give him more. He said, "Oh no Will, that is plenty, I was led to believe that you were quitting right away." When I quit Ross Higgins Co., the manager asked me if I would like a letter of recommendation. I thanked him and told him no. "Well Will," he said, "if you ever do, just drop me a line." A Marine, whom I met when working at Sitka, had since finished his tour and had come to Juneau and obtained a position as book keeper in the firm. He wanted my job, well he got it, and my chum wrote and told me he held it just a week.

I had not been working long on the delivery wagon when a young girl came in and ordered some groceries and said she lived right back of the Catholic Convent. When I got up there, there was only one house back of the Convent so I started up the hill toward it. It had snowed about 6 inches the previous night and as I approached it on the west side I noticed some stairs coming down from a door, but no one had been down them, so went around to the other side and in going noticed that the snow had been melted off of the cover over the chimney. When I reached the north side of the house I saw that the porch had been swept clear of snow but there were no tracks leaving the place, so I went to the door and rapped, thinking that I might get a little information as to where the girl lived. I received no response and naturally figured something was wrong, so put my face to the glass panel, and as I did, noticed the reflection of a man hanging from the rafters. He had got up on the table, tied his own hands so that I could not undo them quickly, then swung off the table. The poor fellow was hanging perfectly listless and still, so that he had been hanging long enough to lose any motion from the swing. I heard later on that I might have saved him. I still think I did the right thing by not trying to revive him even if I could have. He was about 65, no food, no job and what would have been in store for him even if I could have saved him?

Leaving Alaska Forever

A few days before I left Juneau for the States, Geo. Gilmore, who had been in Juneau for a couple of years came to me and said, "Billie, will you do me a favor when you get back to St. Paul?" I told him I would. *[Will was going to St. Paul to study watch repair.]* He asked me to visit his Mother in Minneapolis, who lived at the end of the car line on Hennipen Ave. I told him I would be glad to.

About two weeks after being in St. Paul, I went over to see his Mother. She lived in an old-fashioned plain brick two-story house. I went up to the house, all blinds were down, however finally an elderly lady dressed in black with a bonnet somewhat like the Sisters wear came to the door. I introduced myself and told her I was down from Juneau, Alaska. She said. "Oh I will never see my boy again." I told her he was coming down the following year, which he was counting on doing, but she again repeated that she knew she would never see him again. I tried to console her and told her that quite a lot of the boys from Juneau had come down on the boat as far as Wrangel and Ketchikan, and that he was amongst the ones coming down (which he was) but she still insisted that she would never see him again. I told her we had a good time playing cards and visiting, which was a little far-fetched, as I was coming down as guard with a fellow who had been committed to Mount Tabor, out of Portland, where they cared for the Alaska insane. Well I might as well have touched off a keg of dynamite. She said she had always taught her boy never to touch a card, that it was the devil's own hand. I stood there and tried to patch things up, I told her he really was not playing, but was in the stateroom with the other boys passing the time away. I will admit I lied to her, I would have done anything to have given her peace of mind. I am afraid I failed miserably. Her son Geo. Gilmore died that winter in Juneau.

About six months before I left Juneau, I dreamt one night that I had arrived at my Uncle's house in Willmar, Minn., and two of the girls were upstairs with their Mother and my favorite cousin Marion came to the door and opened it. When I did travel to Willmar I was held up in Minot for several hours. Though I should have reached Willmar about five in the evening, I did not get in until about 2 a.m. so went to the hotel and got a bed, getting up about nine. My visit turned out the way it had been presented to me in Alaska. Since then I have had 14 other such premonitions come to me, which leaves a person wondering about the Great Beyond.

Coming down on the boat, leaving Juneau, and in fact Alaska forever, was the Episcopal minister who took my Dad's place. I was sitting guard outside the cabin doors of the fellow who was being sent to Mt. Tabor, when Rev. Roth came down. He said "Will, I am going to write you a letter of introduction and where ever you settle down I wish you would present it and get interested in church work." He added, "You might have a good influence on someone who might not otherwise resist evil influence." He said that I was the only boy he knew of in Alaska that had not been led astray, or words to that effect. He went on that if he had his way, he would take every friend of his out of Alaska, it was just a stepping stone to hell. I am afraid that I could not quite come up to his high opinion of me as I had at time played some poker, quite a little blackjack and had danced with some of the girls in the dance hall, tho that was as far as I ever went. Liquor did not cross my lips simply because I did not like it.

One Saturday, when I was going to school *[probably in St. Paul]*, I went into Graham's Smoke House, a place where you could buck the cigar machine and play poker if you so desired, and got into a poker game. There was a fellow dressed like a miner who was dealing, when I lost about twenty bucks. I had four aces beat with a straight flush. The City Marshal, a great big 6-2 broad- shouldered fellow, happened in about that time and saw what happened. He said, "Here Billie let me take your hand." I stood there watching and pretty quick he had won about twenty dollars and when he got up from the table turned around to me and said, "Here take this." I told him it wasn't mine, he said you take it. I thought it over and decided my poker playing days were over. I figured I was either going to follow it for a living or quit it, I also thought that in gambling you were the majority of the time taking money from some poor devil that could not afford to lose it, and dealing out misery.

To this day I have only played poker three times, once when I was going down to Wenatchee to play ball in the old steamboat days, when I won enough to pay for my boat fare and another time when my wife and myself were invited out for the evening and I won about thirty-five cents. The third time, I walked into a pool room about 10 p.m. one Thanksgiving evening, there were seven fellows sitting at a table and they asked me to come on take a chair, I told them no thanks, but one fellow said "Oh come on, we need one more to play for a turkey," so I sat down. I won the turkey and gave it to a widow, who kept it until Xmas eve. When she went out to kill it it had died the night before.

[Will's memoirs end here. For the next 70 years he lived an active life in Chelan that is chronicled beginning on p. 141.]

RAILWAYS ACROSS THE WEST

By Paul Magel and Ted Robert Gurr

The first decade of Will Gurr's life was one in which the westward expansion of railways attracted millions of opportunistic immigrants and settlers to the American West. The railways shaped the built landscape of the West and the lives of those who settled and worked there in ways that are difficult to comprehend today. They are part of the background to Will's memoirs, and later to the lives of the people of Chelan and the middle reaches of the Columbia.

The extraordinary railway growth began with the passage of the Pacific Railway Act of 1863. By 1869 the first transcontinental railroad had been completed, permitting travel from New York to San Francisco in only six days. A land grant system, established by the Act and operated by the federal government between 1855 and 1871, made the expansion possible. Hundreds of railway companies were granted huge tracts of land that were uninhabited--except by Native Americans. A total of 129 million acres of federal land and 51 million acres of state land were made available for railroad rights of way or for sale or pledge to bondholders.

The westward expansion of railways stimulated immigration and settlement by an extraordinary variety of people hoping to make new lives away from the crowded cities of the East, and of Europe. Many towns and cities grew out of the rail centers and repair shops that spring up along the routes, and these attracted unskilled and skilled workers as well as merchandisers, saloon keepers, and such professionals as engineers, doctors, lawyers, clergy and teachers. Gamblers, dance hall girls, hucksters and thieves also followed the rails West.

Five major lines linking the West Coast to the East were completed by the early 1890's: *Central,* the Central Pacific, completed in 1869; *South,* the Southern Pacific, completed in 1881 (which took over the

Central Pacific in 1885), and the Santa Fe, completed in 1886; and *North*, the Northern Pacific (1883) and the Great Northern (1893). The Great Northern, built by entrepreneur James Hill, was the only line that did not take advantage of the public land grants.

Will Gurr travelled on each of the three main western rail routes before his tenth birthday. The Rev. Gurr booked a drawing room on the Northern Pacific for the family when Will was five months old, en route to Portland. Celia Gurr's letters, incorporated in the memoirs above, provide a vivid description of rail travel in the mid-1880s. In 1889, following their return from London, Will and his father and brother rode the Southern Pacific (or perhaps the Santa Fe) to San Diego. Will was old enough now to record his own memories of the trip. And in 1893 they rode the original Central Pacific track from California to the World's Fair. After Will's return from Alaska he would have travelled from Seattle to St. Paul and back to Wenatchee on the Great Northern.

The railroads were essential to the lives of the Western towns. They carried freight as well as passengers, including the supplies of shopkeepers like Will Gurr and household goods that ranged from prefabricated buildings to furnishings to foodstuffs. Robert L. Gurr, Will's stepbrother, recalled that one of the staples of lunch at the Gurrland ranch was peanut butter, ordered from Sears in 25 lb. buckets. The growing brood of Henry J. and Mabel Gurr's children was dressed from barrels of second-hand clothing shipped West by missionary societies.

Transport to Chelan was especially difficult until a branch of the Great Northern reached Chelan Falls in 1914. Before then passengers, freight, the peanut butter, and missionary barrels arrived in Wenatchee, were transshipped to Columbia River steamboats, unloaded at Chelan Falls, and then hauled up the steep road to the town. The new Great Northern line went on to Oroville and into Canada, opening up north central Washington State to commerce and passenger travel, and it eventually put the steamboats out of business.

Short-haul railways were a natural extension of the continental routes. They sprouted up everywhere to provide local transportation before the advent of buses, truckers, and private autos. Recall that Will, as a boy in Minnesota, remembers taking a local train a few miles to retrieve sermon notes the Rev. Gurr had left at another parish.

The editor of this book grew up a stone's throw from the Great Northern's maintenance yards in Hillyard, north of Spokane. It was a poor town, though probably better than Will's characterization, a half-century earlier, of Montevideo, Minnesota, another Great Northern rail center, as "one of the toughest little towns I ever in." Hoboes were free-riding passengers on the Western rails and a source of employment for the railroad bulls, the rough men employed to stop them. In Hillyard in the early 1940s hoboes still camped under the abutments of the bridges that passed over the rail yards. And in college I learned the Depression-era song that went, "I know Jim Hill, he's a good friend of mine, that is why I am hiking on Jim Hill's main line. Hallelujah I'm a bum, Hallelujah bum again, Hallelujah give us a handout to revive us again."

Some Westerners still remember the romance of riding the rails in the age of steam. Liz Perry, Chelan's historian, can have the last word on this: "I remember riding the Great Northern steam train to Seattle from Wenatchee. I loved those steam locomotives, it was an adventure."

WILL IN CHELAN 1906-1977
by Ted Robert Gurr

In December 1904, after escorting federal prisoners from Juneau to Seattle, Will used money borrowed from friends to finance a visit to his family in Chelan. The Rev. Henry J. Gurr had arrived there in July 1902 to serve at St. Andrews Church and was to remain for nearly 20 years. The first stage of Will's trip was by rail from Seattle to Wenatchee, then passage on a river boat that boarded at 2 am on December 30th and departed two hours later. By 10am, he said later, the steamboat had made only 60 feet of headway against the Columbia River's strong current and did not complete the 40 mile trip to Chelan Falls until after midnight on December 31. Like other travelers, Will finished the journey on an open horse-drawn sleigh uphill on the old road to Chelan, where the snow was knee-deep. His brother Alf also was in Chelan, visiting their father, and they partied at a New Year's Eve dance until 4:30 am.[25] After a two-day visit Will returned to Seattle and then Juneau.

Two years later Will left Alaska for good. He visited his mother's family in Willmar, Minnesota, at Christmas time in 1906 and then took classes in watch-making in St. Paul. During a visit to his father in Chelan[26] he was impressed by the Lake and decided to stay for a while ... as it turned out, for the next 70 years.

During Will's 70 years in Chelan he became one of the town's leading citizens. He was a businessman downtown for 40 years, pitched

---

25   Alf Gurr stayed in Alaska after the Rev. Gurr and his wife Mabel returned to the lower 48 but made several long visits to Chelan.

26   It is uncertain whether he first stopped in Chelan on his way to Minnesota, or not until afterwards. This chapter incorporates information summarized by Elizabeth Perry, "People Profile – William E. Gurr," *Lake Chelan History Notes*, vol. 19 (2004): 32-35 and notes, documents, and correspondence from the Lake Chelan Museum and the author's files. It also incorporates the recollections of Barbara Van Epps (nee Gibson), the granddaughter of Will's second wife, Gladys Waring Gibson.

for the local baseball team, founded the town's fire department, and served at various times as mayor, council member, deputy sheriff, justice of the peace, and municipal judge before his death in 1977, at age 93. Yet when I visited the Chelan Rotary Club 30 years later, in autumn 2007, only a handful of people recognized his name. What follows is a reconstruction of his life in Chelan.

Opposite: Panoramic view of Chelan town and lower lake, by L.D. Lindsley, 1916. By this time Gurrland had been given up when the family moved closer to town. St. Andrew's Church is across the street from the shops on Woodin Ave, obscured by buildings in the foreground. The Chelan Hotel was built by C. C. Campbell in 1901-02, later renamed the Campbell Hotel, and has been continuously owned and managed by the Campbell family. LCHM

*Will Gurr and Art Campbell in swim suits, 1917. From an enlarge-
ment next to Reception at the Campbell Hotel, reproduced by
permission of the Campbell family.*

A Character Formed in Adversity

Will at 23 was self-confident and self-reliant, character traits shaped by the remarkable experiences of his youth. He also had a moral code instilled in him by his father and reinforced by some of his teachers. He was a skilled sailor, like his father, and adept at other trades from typesetting to cannery work. He also had considerable people skills, as they are called now – he made enduring friendships and impressed many employers. Or so he recalls in his memoirs. And it seems unlikely that he would have been entrusted with so many challenging jobs or charter voyages in Alaska if the praise was exaggerated or undeserved. Rather, as he said in a 1969 letter to his half-brother Robert, he did not want to "look as though I were trying to lay it on, which I do not believe in."

The other side of Will's self-reliance and skills was a degree of self-certainty that bordered on cockiness, often convinced he was right and others wrong. He recounts several "I told you so" episodes in his memoirs, for example about people who sailed on his launch in perilous situations and friends who discounted his advice about hunting. During his years as mayor of Chelan from 1949 to 1952 he reportedly accepted the resignation of all city council members because they would not agree with his policy on hiring and firing city employees. He then appointed all new council members.[27] And he probably instigated a 1927 episode when the 10 members of Chelan's new volunteer fire department, which he had founded, turned in their wrenches to Chief Gurr, saying they would all quit if the city council did not provide them with adequate fire-fighting equipment.[28]

Will remembered and recounted praise from employers in his memoirs, for example the US Marshal in Juneau who said, after his 18

---

27   Personal correspondence from Elizabeth Perry dated September 21, 2004.

28   *Chelan Valley Leader*, April 28, 1927, p. 1.

months service there, that Will was the best guard he ever had. And on Will's last voyage from Alaska the Rev. Roth, an Episcopal priest, told him that he was the only boy he knew of in Alaska that had not been led astray and urged him to consider a career in the ministry. In counterpoint, Will long harbored resentment about those who in his eyes criticized or punished him unjustly. In his memoirs he puts down Juneau employers for paying him too little or rejecting his job applications. In the most remarkable instance, at age nine he was punished for a spitting contest with a California girl, Helen Haley, though she started it, and nearly 40 years later on a visit to San Francisco planned to visit and confront Helen and her mother "in a nice sort of way." Or perhaps Will is spoofing himself here. In any case the plan fell flat because he learned that Helen had died in childbirth.

Two Chelan episodes also suggest an unbending disposition. In 1911 his relative, Captain John Lucas, repeatedly asked if Will would write Clausins' jewelry supply in Spokane so John's son could get a watch at wholesale. Will stalled and then refused, explaining that "I've had trouble with those Clausins, so don't care to write them."[29] And David Hellyer, the executor of his will, told me that Will wanted to be buried in Wenatchee because he did not like the Chelan undertaker.[30] An inherited trait of stubborn pride may be at work here. Will's father, the Rev. Henry J. Gurr, reportedly lost a prosperous member of his struggling St. Andrews Episcopal congregation because, as he told his son Robert, a banker named Van Slyke "took his business to the Methodist Church because I wouldn't go along with a deal to buy his way into heaven."[31]

Will's schooling was episodic. He seems not to have had any instruction in 1890-91 in the San Mateo boarding home, when he was eight and nine. He mentions his step-mother's failure to teach him to read

---

29   "Diary of Captain John B. Lucas – 1911," entries of March 6, 16, and 21. Unpublished transcript, Lake Chelan Historical Society. John Lucas was the father of Mabel Lucas Gurr, the Rev. Gurr's third wife.

30   Personal communication, July 2004. In fact he was buried in Chelan.

31   Notes by David Gurr on a conversation with Robert Gurr in 1970 or 1971.

at this age – she "gave it up as a bad job." He attended a country school in Merced and, probably later the same year, a school in Sonora, where he recalled "readers with stories of adventure, also some with a moral to them which I never forgot." Several years later he was enrolled in schools in Minnesota and, in his late teens, in Juneau. His father had a classical education that included seminary training in Greek and Hebrew and it may be that he gave some attention to teaching his sons. In any case Will acquired the basic three R's, not least those needed to run a small business and to write his memoirs.

The memoirs also show something about Will's attitudes toward the social mosaic of frontier America. His shared his father's acceptance of Negroes, Mexicans, and Indians but also may have been influenced by his father's dislike of Chinese immigrants. In later years he told his granddaughter by marriage, Barbara Van Epps (nee Gibson), that the Chinese railroad workers "worked hard and were poorly treated, and maybe a bit blood-thirsty."[32] In Alaska he worked with Japanese contract laborers with no evident animus, as well as with "Slavs," presumably Russians, and often interacted with native Americans. Will's prejudices were not directed at minorities but at fearful and incompetent men newly arrived in Alaska. He also disliked hop-heads and alcoholics but at the same time was sympathetic to prostitutes – he disapproved of their trade but appreciated their personal qualities.

Will's love of the environment animates many passages in his memoirs. He had a Romantic's appreciation of Alaska's natural beauty and a great fondness for hunting trips into the wilderness, sometimes alone, seldom with more than one companion. In Chelan he was often on the water in a launch that he hired out to carry visitors and supplies up-lake and used for his own camping and hunting trips. Barbara Van Epps remembers that "He did talk of Alaska and enjoyed well-crafted boats all his life. One of the attractions of Chelan was the water." He also loved to hunt and fish and did so

---

32   Personal communication, January 2011. Barbara was five when her grandmother remarried Will in 1957 and was in frequent contact with him for the next half-dozen years. Many of her other recollections of Grandpa Bill, as she called him, are incorporated in the text below.

Lake Chelan from War Creek trail, postcard by Will Gurr   TRG   collection

until his failing sight made them too hazardous. The visual evidence of his naturalism are the many photos he took of the lake and its environs. Most were lost or destroyed after his death but some remain on postcards.

He also kept hunting dogs, according to Barbara, "but they stayed outside and were never pampered and always carefully trained. He did love them and they were a source of pride to him. Later in his life they came into his home more often and were, I believe, good companions. Mike, a Wiemariner, was his last dog and I think his favorite. Mike was the first of his kind I ever met, the breed being little known at the time. Grandpa was a very disciplined and responsible man and I feel Mike was never replaced because Grandpa thought it would be unfair to die and leave a dog behind."

The moral compass of Will's life probably was imbued from his father, a strict and unemotional man who nonetheless was remembered for his small kindnesses to his boys. Will concludes his memoirs by saying that he almost never drank alcohol – because he disliked the taste – nor did he gamble. And while he recounts fond memories of a number of girls and women from his youth, he hints of no sexual adventures.

Will in Business

When Will settled in Chelan in 1906 the town's population was about 600, some of them dry-land farmers and others in businesses that served farm families throughout the region. Some residents worked elsewhere in the Columbia Valley as seasonal harvest hands, others at mines along the lake or, after 1911, at the Wapato Irrigation Project northeast of the lake, on land purchased from Indian allotment holders. The town also had a growing summer tourist trade, mostly vacationers from Pacific Coast cities who stayed at hotels in Chelan or went 55 miles up-lake to a lodge at Stehekin, gateway to the North Cascade wilderness area.

The Rev. Henry J. Gurr had supplemented the meager income provided by his congregation and the Episcopal bishop of Spokane by buying and operating the Chelan Jewelry Co. "which consists of jewelry, optical & stationery departments. " Despite this ambitious description it was housed in a small wooden storefront on the north side of Woodin Avenue in downtown Chelan. In September 1907 he sold a four-fifths interest in the business to Will for $400 plus a promissory note for $220 for future repayment. The Rev. Gurr had been an amateur photographer before and during his years in Alaska and reserved "the privilege of taking the kodak department out of said store" along with photo equipment at any time, with a compensating reduction in Will's indebtedness. [33] There is no evidence that he ever invoked this right – or that Will ever paid the $220.

Will recalled that in his early years in business, during salmon season (before the Chelan Dam was built), the shop owners would take turns minding all the stores while the others went fishing. "Business was slow then and one guy would sit on Woodin Avenue with all the keys, and if a patron came along, he would open the store and get the fellow what he needed. The next day someone else would stay home and do the shopkeeping."[34]

---

33   From a contemporary copy of the contract dated September 28, 1907.
34   From Barbara Van Epp's recollections, January 2011.

Will and friends on Woodin Avenue, ca. 1918. The sidewalks have been paved, the street is still dirt. Mundt's Drug Store is in the background, the placard at right, "The Best of the Good One," may be advertising Sy's bootstore, whose iconic shopsign hangs above the men. WEG album

Under Will's management the jewelry business survived and was moved from one building to another until 1919 when he built a concrete block building faced with brick in the first block of Woodin Avenue and expanded his photo business. Will tried other branches of merchandise as well: a 1927 add in the local paper advertises "Leather Goods... buy a leather billfold, purse, or pocketbook at Gurr's Store." In May 1935 he applied successfully to be appointed the state's liquor vendor for Chelan, after the death of the previous vendor. He moved the $1000 stock of liquor into his jewelry store and announced plans to partition the store with separate entrances to each shop. The 1940 business directory for Chelan lists him as agent for the State Liquor Control Board as well as jeweler.

The Depression hit hard. Will told a newspaper reporter years later that "in three months during the Depression we took in $226 and I think 65 cents...No, it was rough! We were $10,000 in the hole."[35] In 1948, when Will was 65, he sold the business to Daryl Nutley, a long-time friend from their days on the fire department.

---

35   Transcript of an interview by Daryl Curtis, January-February 1972, in the Lake Chelan Museum files, p. 6.

Chelan's pennant-winning baseball team, 1916, Will middle row at right

LCHM

Will in Baseball

There's no evidence from Will's account of his California and Alaska years that he was interested or skilled in sports, other than hunting, yet he was and remained in good physical shape almost all his life. He got around Chelan on his bicycle, even after his eyesight failed. In the summer he swam in the lake almost daily. Barbara Van Epps remembers that in his 60's he would walk or ride to her father's Chelan Airways dock, put on a white bathing cap, swim to a point about a mile uplake, and then back. "He made quite a picture, but he was respected by everyone, and I never heard a negative comment."

As a young man baseball gave Will an entry into Chelan community life. Elizabeth Perry observes that "By the 1870s almost every town in the United States had its amateur team to give pride and unity" to the community. In Chelan, as elsewhere, players were local and there were no franchises or salaries or paid admissions. Chelan put together its first town team about 1907 and the *Leader* recounts its victories and losses in contests with teams from other communities along the Columbia. Rosters compiled by Elizabeth Perry list Will on the team from 1910 through 1916 – the records are incomplete.

The competitive and community nature of town baseball must have appealed to him. He recalled playing in the nearby towns of Waterville, a farm town about 15 miles south on the east side of the Columbia, and Pateros, about 20 miles up the river. "I know I went up in the early days to play ball at Waterville and we had to get off the wagon for 50-60 feet and push it up there." The Chelan team would play in Pateros on alternate Sundays and the Pateros team would come down to Chelan the following Sunday.[36]

---

36   Curtis interview, pp. 5, 6.

In 1913 the Chelan Town Team took the name of the Giants and in 1914 finished at the bottom of the local league. By 1916 they won its pennant. Will played a number of positions during these years but mainly as pitcher, being caught by Louie Wapato, an Indian from Wapato Point.[37] In a 1974 interview Will reminisced that he had been on the team when they went to play in Wenatchee. The team "stopped at Douglas County and loaded wheat sacks and played poker and won enough for round trip tickets." In Wenatchee they stayed in an old bedbug-infested hotel. "Next day I pitched. Joe Wilkinson was coach. Bob Harris couldn't catch the ball and we got beat 15-1. Duffy, the Wenatchee coach, gave us a bottle of beer."[38] A bottle each, one hopes.

---

37   Elizabeth Perry, "Baseball – Chelan Town Team," *History Notes*, Published by the Lake Chelan History Society, vol. 19 (2004), 21-30. The Wapato family, who owned substantial allotments, were frequent participants in Chelan community events. The *Leader*, in its account of the July 4 celebrations of 1911, said that "Long Jim, the stately, dignified hereditary chief of the Chelan Indians, attended the celebration this week and entered some of his horses in the races."

38   Excerpts from a taped interview dated 1974, provided by Elizabeth Perry.

Chelan's 1st Volunteer Fire Dept. 1926-27   Curr Photo

Will and the Fire Department

Western towns in the early 20th century were built almost entirely of wood. Fire safety inspections and the use of fire retardant materials were decades in the future. Fires were frequent and, when driven by wind, could devastate entire business districts. Chelan is on the dry eastern slope of the Cascades and gets relatively little rain – which increased the fire risks. Will recalled that when he arrived in town the public water supply was a 2" pipe running up the center of the street, probably Woodin Avenue.

A volunteer group of fire fighters had formed in Chelan in 1916 but there was no regular fire department until Will organized one in 1926. By the time the department was established there were regular water lines and some hydrants. The photo opposite is from the Lake Chelan Historical Museum, dated 1926-28. It shows Will (at left) and ten men in fire-fighting clothing standing next to a fire truck, evidence that the City Council had provided them some resources. In a 1972 interview Will recalled a number of serious fires in Chelan. "The Auditorium was really the worst fire we had. We lost the City Hall, the Jail, and a house on the corner where I think Doctor Mitchell lived. Anyway, it wiped that out and it jumped across the street and set the Anthony building afire about four times. I was on the nozzle on the hose located between the Auditorium and Anthony's and I'd keep playing the hose back on the Anthony building and then throw it on the Auditorium again."³⁹

Fire fighting in the early 20th century was at least as dangerous as it is now because fire fighters had little or no training and not much equipment. Will came close to losing his life when fighting a fire at a warehouse in Chelan Falls, a tall building between the river and the railroad tracks. This is an edited version of Will's recollections:

---

39   From the Curtis interview, p. 12. No date is given for this fire or the Chelan Falls warehouse fire described in the following account.

"We got a call from a fellow that worked for the Washington Water Power, he got up during the night to go to the bathroom, looked out the window, and happened to see the whole roof raise on the warehouse down at the Falls. He called the department and we went down there. Mike Harris had been on the Spokane Fire Department so I thought he might know something about handling a warehouse fire so I asked him how he would handle it and he says, 'I'll be darned if I know.'

"So I set out to walk around the building and said, 'Mike, you or George put that smoke mask on, will you, put the rope around you, and go in there and see if you can open that door.' The door was 30 feet along the side. After I walked around the building sizing it up, and just as I came around the corner, I heard Mike say to George, 'I'll be damned if I've lost anything in there, have you?' George said no. So I told Mike to get the fire extinguisher and the smoke mask and I tied the rope around me and put the mask on.

"The smoke in there was awful thick but I went in and headed to where I thought the side door was. I got over to the wall and ran my hand along and couldn't feel any casing, but I hit a club 'bout that long that was hanging there on a leather thong. I started down then to the lower side of the warehouse, the downriver side, and the floor started to give under me. I backed up then and knew where the fire was. I went outside and told the boys just rip the lower boards off the building, in that corner, and wash it out. And that's the way we got it.

"Then I went up to the roof and was walking along – I was on the land side, which was frozen, though the side toward the river didn't freeze at all - and my feet went out from under me. A man and a woman were standing on the track, watching me, and I suppose the fire boys below, and the woman saw me fall. We had placed a fire ladder on that side of the building and, as luck would have it, as I went over the edge I was just able to reach out and grab the top of it. She hollered at some of the firemen underneath, 'Grab that ladder!' As I went over I caught one rung and when I swung over got ahold of another, and saved myself. But I pulled the ladder over about 5 feet and as luck would have it, two of the heaviest boys on the department happened to be holding it – Less Bumgarner and Harry Varney. If it hadn't been for them I'd have been cooked.

"Later on I was on the river side checking. We had a little portable water pump and it started to miss, so I started down to it because I knew more about handling it than anybody. George Givens, who was down there, found out the gas tank was empty so he took the gasoline can, filled and overflowed the tank, and set the whole works on fire. I carried a two-and-a-half gallon fire extinguisher on the running board of my pickup so I grabbed that and when I used the last drop I had the fire killed in the gas tank. But the carburetor was still afire, so I grabbed the hat off my head and smothered it. That's how close we came to losing the building."

And we can count three times when Will 's life was at risk on that fire: when the burning floor began to buckle beneath him, when he fell from the roof, and when the pump caught fire. At the beginning of his narrative Will mentions that the warehouse was insured for $10,000 and cost $2,500 to repair. He also says the fire was set but never elaborates. [40]

---

40   From the Curtis interview, pp. 8-10.

Will in Public Office

We know almost nothing of Will's thoughts about events in the world outside Chelan. He lived through two world wars and the Great Depression, but, aside for the latter's effects on his business, there are no records of how he was affected, if at all. None of his correspondence between his arrival in Chelan and the 1960s has survived. In his later correspondence, though, he never refers to larger political or economic issues and he may not have done so in earlier years.

Will was active in local politics and government for most of his adult life. He was a member of the Chelan city council from 1914 to 1916, and maybe later. For a decade from 1918 to 1928 he was deputy sheriff, with one surviving record of an arrest. In June 1923, he found 220 gallons of corn mash in the house of one Peter St. Luise. Peter was fined $250 for operating an illegal still and sentenced to 60 days in jail.[41] After organizing the Fire Department in 1926, Will remained as chief for eight years. He also was justice of the peace and municipal judge, though the records do not say when. And he was elected mayor in 1949 and served to 1952, when he was 69 years old.

It is not likely that Will's public service was motivated by political ambition. Rather, a man of his reputation and ability was expected to serve the community. And perhaps, given what we know of his character, he thought he was better able to do so than most of his peers. Aside from his recollections about firefighting the only story worth telling about any of years in public office has already been told: when serving as mayor he accepted the resignation of the entire city council in a dispute over city employees. Other accounts remain to be be found in microfiche copies of the *Chelan Valley Leader* and its successor, the *Chelan Valley Mirror*.

---

41   *Chelan Valley Leader,* June 23, 1923.

Maude and Will Gurr on horseback early in their marriage   *WEG*
album

Two Marriages and Two Deaths

In May 1909 Will married 21-year-old Maude Pruett at her home, with Judge C. C. Campbell officiating and only two friends as guests. Maude was the daughter of early settlers in the wheat country of southeast Washington, Robert and Mary Pruett. After they separated Mary Pruett and several of their children moved to Chelan in 1902 where she operated a boarding house called the Home Restaurant and Lodging House on Woodin Avenue. She later changed the name to Hotel Pruett.

Maude worked at her mother's hotel serving meals, which may be where she and Will met. She had been married before, in June 1906. It was a brief marriage to one William Green and probably annulled, as Maude resumed using her maiden name of Pruett. We know virtually nothing about her 43-year marriage to Will except that it ended in her death in 1952 after a long bout with cancer. Contemporary census records say she has no occupation – no euphemisms like home-maker were used. In a letter written years later Will mentions that he and Maude often would go to the Chelan House, later known as the Campbell Hotel "with two other couples, clear away the tables in the dining room, and dance."[42] Aside from that reference there is no contemporary correspondence, newspaper items, or even family anecdotes. "Herstory," like that of most other women of her time and place, was a blank page.

In 1954, two years after Maude's death, Will married Gladys Waring Gibson. He was 71, she about 62. We know from census records that she and her first husband, Arthur Gibson, had lived in Maryland, Missouri, and Aberdeen, Washington, before she was widowed and moved to Chelan. Will acquired two stepsons, one of them 36-year-old Ernie Gibson, a wartime flying instructor who in 1953 (or 1957 – sources differ) bought and operated Chelan Airways. The Airways' float planes provided passenger service from the Chelan waterfront to Stehekin and Lucerne, the lake-side landing of the Howe Sound Mine.

---

42   Letter dated August 7, 1972, to Father Jack Gurr.

Maude and Will Gurr at home, ca. 1940   *TRG collection*

Ernest and his wife Edith had three children, of whom Barbara was the youngest. Will had no children of his own but after his marriage to Gladys he grew close to Barbara. She recalls visiting her Grandma, learning to crochet, and "often Grandpa would come home for lunch and admire our needle work." He also taught her about fishing and gardening. Barbara recalls:

"I remember him taking me fishing a few times, teaching me to cast my line, reel the line in at just the right speed, patiently wait for the second gut on the line before I set the hook. I was always in a hurry and jerked the hook too soon, losing the fish more often than not. Grandpa remained patient. One day he took me and my Grandma out to Lake Perrigan....We rented a boat and were trolling for trout. I was hopeless with the gear, constantly tangling the long lines of lures and reeling in with no fish in sight. Fortunately Grandpa was able to catch enough fish to make the trip worthwhile, and was as happy as me when I managed to catch a surprisingly large fish.

"He was also one of the first 'organic gardeners.' He had a small garden at the front of a tiny house one door down from us on Nixon Avenue. He kept a compost pile which sometimes smelled a bit rotten but he grew tasty tomatoes and other vegetables. He also grew mint, comfrey, chamomile and other herbs he used for tea and poultices. I once skinned one of my fingers and it took on the look of infection setting in. He made a poultice and wrapped my finger in what I think was a comfrey leaf and the very next day my finger was much improved.

"He had planted and maintained beautiful roses for my Grandma at the home where my Dad and I lived [after Barbara's parents divorced]. He was unwilling to let them suffer the fate of forgottenness, and showed up at the house one morning with loppers, aphid-spray and a small saw. He sat me down on the couch with paper and pen and instructed me on the care and feeding of roses, and I did write down everything he said. He taught me the difference between the Tea Roses and the Floribundas and how each should be pruned, what to spray, and when. Then we went outside and together, on our hands and knees, we pruned a dozen rose bushes....His favorite rose was the Mirandy, a dark red rose with velvety petals, perfect from bud to full bloom, and the proper smell for a rose."[43]

Barbara also remembers that when she graduated from high school in 1970, "Grandpa Bill gave me the most beautiful white gold watch....He brought three of them to the house for me to choose from....All were beautiful, the one I chose was flower shaped and I have yet to see a prettier one." He also gave her a children's novel, *Captain January* (a children's book by Laura E. Richards, first published in 1891), inscribed "William Gurr – From Holy Trinity [Juneau] Sunday School Christmas 1900."

Gladys died in 1963 after nine years of their marriage, a victim of breast cancer. Will lived alone for the last 15 years of his life, though he did take in a housemate in his declining years. For a while he remained close to other members of the Gibson family. Barbara recalls that

---

43   Personal correspondence, January 2011.

Gladys Waring Gibson and Will Gurr, late 1950s   *WEG album*

"When I was 15 [in 1967] my mom was in a car accident and suffered a broken neck. Grandpa rode with us on two occasions to visit her. When I entered the room I was stunned to see my mom with a weird contraption screwed onto her shaved head. I stood speechless for a very long moment, until Grandpa came behind me, put his hand on my shoulder and whispered, 'Barbie, go kiss your mother.' I did as he asked and felt better immediately. Later he said that he felt she was nervous and needed it. He was really very kind in thought and deed."

"My mom did quite a bit of his correspondence for him before she left my Dad. Grandpa had intended to leave the house he lived in, next to ours, and the house next to it, to my Dad. Unfortunately, after they divorced when I was about 20, my mother ended up with all the houses. The house we lived in was originally my Grandma and Grandpa's; he split it into a duplex so my Dad and Mom had a place to live when they came to Chelan."

Later Will's relations with the Gibson family became strained, for what reason we do not know. In a letter dated September 27, 1971, his sister-in-law Anne Gurr (my mother) wrote that "He seems to have no contact with the Gibsons - he mentioned that Mrs. Gibson [presumably the second wife of Ernie Gibson] used to do his washing but she got too busy. There seems to be some friction there – he mentioned that she had a photo album of his but when he asked for it she said she had lost it." This may be the album that Barbara found and shared with me in 2011.

Will with his bicycle, mid-1970s. This photo accompanied his obituary in the Chelan Valley Leader *of May 18, 1977*   *LCHM*

Declining Years

His eyesight began to fail Will in his late 80's, though he continued to use his bicycle to get around town. Anne Gurr described a visit to Will in September 1971.

"He seemed very glad to have us, and was a most generous host. While we took the trip up the lake he stayed home and prepared a lovely dinner of chicken and rice and blueberry pie....Will says his sight has deteriorated considerably this summer....He still rides his bicycle but says he cannot see a car head on, only by looking out of the side of his eye....he is finding it difficult to eat, his close vision is the worst. He keeps house after a fashion but only goes through the motions and really needs a person to come in once a week and clean, but he is so independent, I feel he will not admit to outsiders his helplessness."[44]

Will kept up correspondence with family members until shortly before his death in 1977, writing in an increasingly shaky longhand after 1970. His correspondence often incorporates stories from his memoirs as well as more mundane accounts about Chelan's weather, articles he has read about Alaska, and work on his house at 127 E. Nixon Street. The last suggests that he was far from helpless. Despite age and infirmity he continued to do major maintenance, saying in a May 1975 letter to Father Jack that "In the last year I spent about a thousand dollars insulating the building, putting in 220 for an electric heater and paying part on a Stainless Steel double sink, having the two carpets cleaned, and other incidentals. Right now am starting to paint the house ... at least three walls need it. Scrape the paint today and plan to paint tomorrow."

---

44   Letter from Anne Gurr to Father Jack, September 27, 1971.

Last Will and Testament

By early 1977 Will was failing. Barbara recalls that "There had been some incident which landed him in the nursing home. I am not sure, but experiences since have made me suspect a sundowners-like episode. My Dad [Ernie Gibson] truly loved and respected Bill and visited him every night after work. I went with him a few times, on the last visit I remember him sitting on his bed, very calm and dignified, stating that he could not understand why he had done what he did, he had not been feeling well, regardless he was sure it would not happen again, and he would like to return to his home. My Dad told him if that was what he wanted, it was his decision and we would make it happen."

It was not to happen. "His condition deteriorated rapidly and my next and last visit with Grandpa Bill was at the hospital. He was in a coma. I could think of nothing to say, so I took his hand and said the Lord's Prayer, kissed his forehead and said goodbye."

Will died on May 12, 1977, in Chelan Community Hospital after four months of care. The immediate cause of death was pneumonia, the contributing factor – according to Dr. William Danke – chronic mild cerebral arteriosclerosis. His funeral, four days later, was held at St. Andrews. The church was filled with mourners, even sitting in the choir chairs and as many folding chairs as could be fitted in. He was buried in an embossed coffin at Riverview Cemetery next to the grave of Maude, his first wife – though the actual interment was delayed because the gravediggers struck rock. It seems a fitting resting place for Will, a grave that had to be blasted from rock even more resilient than he was. [45]

Will's will showed that he had property worth about $11,000 and a small bank account. He had already dispersed some of his possessions, for example two TVs that he gave away when he could no lon-

---

45   From his death certificate; and a postcard from my mother, Anne Gurr, who attended the funeral.

ger see them. To his half-brother Robert and half-sister Harriett he bequeathed $1.00 each "and my love and affection." To his half-sister Helen, living in the San Francisco Bay area, he bequeathed $200, not that he was close to her but more likely because she was living in hard circumstances. Robert Nichols evidently shared Will's house on Nixon Avenue for a time because Will left him a $300 bond and most of the house's kitchen furnishings. His stepson Ernest Gibson inherited much of his residual estate as well as many odds and ends of household goods, a Colt .32 handgun, a filing cabinet, and "all pictures." In a 2004 visit to Chelan I was unable to learn what had happened to the pictures or the contents of the filing cabinet. So I have had to rely on family correspondence and items in the Lake Chelan Museum archives.[46]

L ocal people in Chelan remembered Will as a rather quiet man who enjoyed a joke and visiting with friends. Barbara says "he was a gentleman, always." He also had a strong sense of family. Even after his eyesight began to fail he kept up a voluminous correspondence with relatives, some of whom were regular visitors to Chelan. He fathered no children, despite two marriages, but treated the grandchildren he inherited from his second wife as though they were his own. Barbara recalls that he spent many hours telling her stories about his Alaskan adventures and not until she was 11 or 12 did she learn that he was not her real grandfather – "and knowing the truth changed nothing." It is likely that Will intended his memoirs as a legacy to Barbara and her two brothers, and to his more distant relatives – including his nephew, the editor of these memoirs. Now the stories of his early life can be shared more widely.

---

46   With thanks to David Hellyer, attorney, who gave me a copy of the will and also shared his memories of Will Gurr's last years.

Made in the USA
Charleston, SC
02 September 2011